THE STORY OF

TECUMSEH

BY

NORMAN S. GURD

" They are dead, their cause is lost,
their enemies have written their
history."

TORONTO
WILLIAM BRIGGS
1912

Upper Canada Press

An imprint of

American History Press

Franklin, Tennessee

www.Americanhistorypress.com

www.Americanhistoryimprints.com

ISBN 13: 978-0-9842256-7-5

ISBN 10: 09842256-7-6

Original copyright Canada, 1912, by

The Deputy Minister of Education, Ontario

This is an April 2010 b/w facsimile reprint of the original 1912

edition with a new index

Library of Congress Control Number:

2010905269

Printed in the United States of America on acid-free paper

This book meets all ANSI standards for archival quality

TO

THE MEMORY OF

Thaddeus W. H. Leavitt

SOMETIME INSPECTOR OF PUBLIC LIBRARIES
FOR ONTARIO

" Surely somewhere afar
In the sounding labor house vast
Of being is practised that strength
Zealous, beneficent, firm."

.

PREFACE

Less than a century has elapsed since the death of Tecumseh, but in that short period of time the figure of the great Shawanoe chief has become shadowy and unreal. The place and date of his birth are uncertain, his burial-place is unknown. No authentic portrait has come down to us, and the descriptions of his appearance are varied and contradictory. To the Indians he has become a hero as legendary as Hiawatha. He is remembered by Canadians as the leader of the Indian allies of the Crown in the war of 1812, but few realize the extent of his services to Canada in her hour of need.

It is natural that little should be known concerning Tecumseh's early life. He lived with his tribe in the wilderness to the north of the Ohio River, then almost wholly Indian territory, where he conceived his great plan of forming a confederacy of the Indians for the purpose of resisting the encroachment of the white men on the Indian lands. It was part of his policy to remain in the background, preferring that his brother, Tenkswatawa, should appear to be the leader of the movement. Indeed, as late as 1810, he is described in despatches sent by Colonel Elliott to Major-General Brock as " Tecumseh, the brother to the Shawanoe Prophet."

Not until 1811 did the Americans awaken to the fact that Tecumseh was the leading spirit in the Indian

Preface

League. Then he first began to assume importance in the eyes of his enemies and to occupy a place in the history of the Border Wars. After the disaster at Tippecanoe, Tecumseh tried in vain to rally his followers in support of their common cause. It was then that in despair he offered his services to the British King.

Tecumseh appeared in Canada on the eve of the War of 1812. Events succeeded each other so rapidly in that desperate struggle that historians of the period make but brief mention of the heroic chief who was to them but one of many players in the great drama then being enacted.

From what has been said, it will be apparent to the reader how difficult is the task of the writer who would tell the story of Tecumseh. Drake's " Tecumseh " is the standard, and practically the only, work on the subject, but the later chapters are really a history of the War of 1812, not a biography of the chief. The writer is aware that the same criticism may be made of his own work. He can only say that during the past three years he has sought material from every available source. Scores of books and official documents have been consulted. He has visited the scenes of Tecumseh's life, conversed with the descendants of the early settlers, and heard from the lips of the red men the traditions concerning Tecumseh handed down in their tribes. In the following pages he has tried to depict for young Canadians the noble and pathetic figure of this hero of a lost cause.

NORMAN GURD.

Sarnia, Ont., 1911.

CONTENTS

LIST OF ILLUSTRATIONS

NOTE.—For full description of above illustrations see Appendix, page 186.

THE BATTLE OF TIPPECANOE.

(From the original painting by Chappel)

THE STORY OF TECUMSEH

CHAPTER I.

THE BIRTH OF TECUMSEH.

In the latter part of the eighteenth century there stood on the banks of the Mad River (a tributary of the Ohio), about seven miles below the site of the present city of Springfield, a village of the Shawanoe Indians, called Piqua. This village had been built on the site of an ancient Indian town known as "Chilicothe." Near the river, the banks of which at this point were about twenty feet high, stood a rude fort, built of logs and surrounded by a stockade of cedar pickets. Outside the stockade were grouped the huts and wigwams of the inhabitants, and surrounding the village were the cornfields and orchards. Looking to the southward there met the eye a stretch of prairie-land hemmed in by the forest. On this prairie roamed occasional herds of buffalo, wanderers from the great plains of the West. Deer and antelope were to be seen in great numbers, feeding on the rich prairie grass. Beyond the village to the westward lay the unbroken forest. On the north the land was rough and broken, rising abruptly into rocky cliffs. Here and there a dwarfed cedar or pine clung to the face of the precipice with gnarled and twisted roots, or a hardy vine hung its

The Story of Tecumseh

green curtain over the naked rock. To the eastward ran the Mad River in its impetuous descent to the Ohio.

Amid these scenes the young Tecumseh was born in the year 1768. His father, Puckeshinwau, was a chief of the Kiscopoke, and his mother, Methoataske, a member of the Turtle band, both clans of the Shawanoe tribe, which was itself a sub-tribe of the great Algonquin nation. The name, Tecumseh, the primary meaning of which is " a panther springing upon its prey," also signifies a shooting star, the vivid imagination of the Indians picturing a falling star as the panther of the sky.

Tecumseh was the fourth child, and three other children were born after him. Cheeseekau, the eldest of the family, achieved some fame as a warrior. Laulewasikaw, later known as " the Prophet," was closely associated with Tecumseh throughout his life. Of the other members of the family little is known save their names. According to the Indian custom, the young Tecumseh, immediately after his birth, was placed in a sack made of soft deerskin, laced up the front with leather thongs and decorated with embroidery of coloured quills. This was strapped to a flat board having a wooden bow extending over the infant's head. Even though she was the wife of the chief, Tecumseh's mother had little time to devote to her child. She must gather firewood, prepare and cook the food brought in by the hunters, make and mend the deerskin clothing and moccasins, cure the skins of deer and other animals, and sow and cultivate and reap their little harvest of Indian corn.

For the first year of his life the little Tecumseh was

The Birth of Tecumseh

carried about by his mother in the odd little cradle strapped to her back. When she worked in the fields she would place the cradle against a tree, or pass the loop over a branch so that the cradle might swing to and fro in the breeze. After the little lad was a year old he was fed on soup made of venison or fish, thickened with wild rice or corn. In the fall the Indian women gathered the rice and stored it for food during the long winter months. Paddling their canoes into the marsh, they would pull the rice stalks over the side and thresh out the grain with the paddles into the bottom until the frail crafts were loaded as deep as safety permitted. Thousands of wild ducks came to feed on the rice. Disturbed by the canoes, they rose, their wings sounding like thunder, and whirling in the air betook themselves to the deeper solitudes of the marshes. Passenger pigeons flew northward in the spring, and returned southward again in the fall in such vast numbers that the sun was darkened at mid-day.

It was a very wonderful and interesting world to the young Tecumseh. He was soon able to run about the village and to ask countless questions about everything he saw or heard. His schooldays had begun. Yet he did not study out of books. His teachers were his parents and elder brothers. From them he learned the names of the plants and trees and how they were useful to man. He learned, too, the names of the animals and their habits. Walking through the woods his father would tell him what animals had passed, and how long since they had gone by. It was easy to read the tracks in the snow,

The Story of Tecumseh

but hard to decipher the trail in the summer woods. He learned

> " How the beavers built their lodges,
> Where the squirrels hid their acorns,
> How the red deer ran so swiftly,
> Why the rabbit was so timid."

Of the birds he

> " Learned their names and all their secrets,
> How they built their nests in Summer,
> Where they hid themselves in Winter."

Like all Indian children, Tecumseh had to shift more or less for himself. In and out through the village he went, swimming in the river, creeping through the forest in some mimic war-play, watching the building of canoes, greeting the hunters on their return from the chase—here, there and everywhere, full of the boundless energy which goes with a happy heart in a strong and healthy young body. He watched the women stretching the fresh skins of the deer, flesh side uppermost, on the ground by pegs driven in the edges. He saw them scrape off the fat, and rub in salt to preserve the skin, and the brains of the animal to make the leather soft and pliable. Thus he learned how the animals supplied him with clothing as well as food.

He joined the other boys in their play, shooting his tiny arrows at the birds and squirrels, or, what he liked best of all, playing at war. In the winter evenings as he sat by the fire, wrapped in warm furs, listening to the howling of the north wind through the forest, his mother

The Birth of Tecumseh

would tell him old Indian tales and legends. She told
him that long ago the world was covered with water, so
that not even the highest hills were visible. Wisukateak,
who was a great magician, saved himself from the flood
by building a raft. The beaver, the otter and the muskrat climbed upon the raft. Wisukateak said to the beaver,
" Go down to the bottom and see if you can bring up a
little earth." The beaver dived deep under the water,
and after a long time came to the surface dead. Then
Wisukateak said to the otter, " Go down to the bottom
and see if you can bring up a little earth." But the otter,
too, came up and floated dead on the water. Then Wisukateak said to the little muskrat, " Go down to the
bottom and see if you can bring up a little earth." The
muskrat remained under the water a very long time, and
when he came up, he, too, was dead, but in his claws was a
little mud. Then Wisukateak restored the three animals
to life, and taking the mud brought up by the muskrat,
rolled it into a little ball and laid it on the raft. He then
blew upon it and the ball became very large. Then Wisukateak said to the wolf, " My brother, run around the
world, and see how large it is." The wolf ran around the
world, and after a long time came back, and said, " The
world is very large." But Wisukateak thought the world
was still too small, so he blew again and made it much
larger. Then he said to the crow, " Fly around the world
and see how large it is." But the crow never came back,
so Wisukateak decided that the world was large enough.

The little Tecumseh watched the flashing northern
lights in the cold winter sky. His mother told him that

The Story of Tecumseh

these were the spirits of the departed dancing the ghost dances as they journeyed to the happy hunting-grounds. He loved to hear the old, old Indian fairy tale of Shingebiss, the brave little duck. Shingebiss lived in a tiny wigwam near a northern lake. He prepared four logs that he might have fire in his lodge through the four cold winter months—one log for each month. Every morning Shingebiss left his lodge and went out on the frozen lake. When he came to the rushes he pulled them out with his strong bill, and diving through the hole in the ice, caught many fish. The North Wind watched Shingebiss, and was angry to see how little he cared for the cold, so the North Wind blew stronger and stronger, and sent the snow to cover the land deeper and deeper. Yet Shingebiss was not frightened, but caught fish as before. Then the North Wind was still more angry. He came himself and stood at the doorway of Shingebiss's lodge, and the biting air crept in and the wigwam crackled with the cold, but Shingebiss only laughed and stirred the fire, saying:

> "Windy god, I know your plan,
> You are but my fellow-man.
> Blow you may your coldest breeze,
> Shingebiss you cannot freeze.
>
> "Sweep the strongest wind you can,
> Shingebiss is still your man.
> Hey! for life, and Ho! for bliss,
> Who so free as Shingebiss?"

Then the North Wind came into the wigwam and sat by the fire, but little Shingebiss did not seem to notice him.

16

The Birth of Tecumseh

He only stirred the fire till the flames leaped up in the air, and sang more loudly his brave little song. Presently it was too hot for the North Wind, so he left the lodge and went away.

At night when Tecumseh lay sleepless, looking up through the smoke-hole in the wigwam at the stars twinkling in the sky, he thought of brave little Shingebiss. Even when he was frightened he did not cry at night. His mother had told him that bad Indians might hear him and come out of the dark forest. The hoot of an owl might be the signal to hidden foes. He never heard it at night without a quickened beating of the heart. The night breeze, laden with the scent of the sleeping woods, softly moving the flap of the wigwam, startled him, but he made no outcry. Was he not the son of a chief, and was he not to be a great warrior himself? So he would fall asleep, to be awakened by the early rays of the sun and the stir of life about the camp.

The Story of Tecumseh

CHAPTER II.

THE WAMPUM KEEPER.

THE old log fort possessed a singular fascination for the young Tecumseh. Almost daily he made his way through the gate of the palisade and ascended the wall of the fort. Below in the courtyard was the mouth of the well from which water was drawn in time of siege; raised above the ground were bins containing a store of corn for the support of the garrison. In the fort were stored bows and arrows and spears against the time of need. Sitting on the ramparts in the twilight of a summer evening, Tecumseh dreamed of a day to come when the enemy would emerge from the forest. He pictured the invaders creeping nearer and nearer the fort, and then, when discovered, charging the stockade. In imagination he heard the twang of the bow-string, the crackle of musketry, the hissing of bullets, and over all the mingled sounds of battle the wild and terrible war-cry. He fancied himself a warrior shouting defiance, sending his death-dealing arrows among the foe, or hard pressed, tomahawk in hand, rallying the defenders for a last stand against the enemy swarming over the defences.

He loved to talk with Passitotha, the old wampum keeper, who lived within the confines of the fort. The old historian of the tribe told him many tales of battles fought long ago and of the great deeds of his warrior

The Wampum Keeper

ancestors. Tecumseh was permitted to touch and handle the wampum belts as he listened to the story of the event which each commemorated. The oldest belt had been sent from the far South at the time the Spaniards first landed in America. The message had been that something white had been seen on the sea approaching the shore. At first it was thought to be a great bird, but as it drew nearer the Indians perceived that it was an immense canoe. Out of this canoe came a strange animal, half man, half quadruped (a mounted horseman), and this animal commanded the thunder and lightning. Other belts commemorated treaties made with other tribes of Indians, or with the French or English.

The venerable wampum keeper told the young Tecumseh the history of the Shawanoe people, as preserved in the legends of the tribe. He told how the Master of Life, who was himself an Indian, made the Shawanoes before any other of the human race. They came from his brain, and he gave them all the knowledge he possessed. All the other red men were descended from the Shawanoes. The Master of Life made the English and French out of his breast, and the Dutch out of his feet. Long ago the ancestors of the Shawanoes inhabited a foreign land which they had determined to leave. They gathered their people together and marched to the seashore. Here they halted to choose a leader. After the principal men had declined the duty, a member of the Turtle tribe accepted the chieftainship. Placing himself at the head of his people, he walked into the sea, which miraculously divided, and over the bed of the ocean the Shawanoes

The Story of Tecumseh

journeyed to this land (America). After the Shawanoes had come to this island and while they were yet exploring the land, they camped in the midst of a great forest. At night they saw through the trees the reflection of a fire. Curiosity overcoming their fear, they made their way through the woods towards the light. Presently they came to a cleared space, in the midst of which a great fire was burning. The Shawanoes stood under the trees without the circle, not daring to venture closer. After the flames had died down, they observed a movement in the ashes and heard a great puffing sound. Suddenly a man stood up and walked out of the fire. This was the first man of the Piqua band, the name meaning "He who comes out of the ashes." For a time the tribe lived on the shores of Lake Erie, but just before the white men came to these shores, the Iroquois fell upon the Shawanoes, and after many battles drove them from their country. Some of the tribes fled westward, where they lost their identity as Shawanoes, and became known as the Kickapoos. Others fled southward. Continually harassed by the Iroquois, they found no refuge from their inveterate foe until they reached Florida.

Though few in numbers the Shawanoes were a proud and warlike race. They soon came into conflict with the southern tribes, the Creeks and Cherokees. Driven from Florida, they moved northward toward their old home. For a time they halted on the banks of the Savannah River in the territory of the Delawares. The Shawanoes built their village nearly opposite to one of the Delaware villages. They did not, however, remain long in the land

The Wampum Keeper

of the Delawares. One day the women and children of
both tribes were gathering berries near the Delaware village. The younger children were playing in the open
spaces near the river, chasing the butterflies and shooting
their tiny arrows at the birds. One of the Shawanoe children chased and caught a very large grasshopper, and
proudly showed it to his companions. The Delaware
children claimed that the wonderful grasshopper belonged
to them, as it had been caught on the Delaware side of
the river. Very soon the children were fighting over the
grasshopper. The women, hearing the crying and shouting, came to inquire what was the matter, and soon themselves came to blows. Being more numerous, the Delaware women drove their opponents to the canoes. The
Shawanoe squaws retreated to their village, followed by
the derisive shouts of the Delawares. As soon as the
Shawanoe hunters returned to camp, they were surrounded
by the excited women and children, who told of the in-
sults and injuries they had suffered at the hands of the
Delawares, and clamoured for revenge. The Shawanoe
braves launched their canoes and set out for the Delaware
village. The Delawares were ready and advanced to meet
the foe. The odds were much against the Shawanoes, and
after a desperate battle in which many were slain on both
sides, the remnant of the Shawanoes took to flight. This
battle was called the Grasshopper War.

Abandoning their village on the Savannah, the Shawanoes journeyed northward to the valley of the Ohio, " The
beautiful river," and there built new villages where they
have ever since dwelt in comfort and security.

21

The Story of Tecumseh

CHAPTER III.

THE COUNCIL FIRE

ONE morning the young Tecumseh, pretending that he was a warrior on the trail of an enemy, stalked down a pathway into the woods. With his little tomahawk in his hand he stole along the trail, now gliding noiselessly behind a tree trunk in mock alarm, and again stealthily emerging when the threatened danger had passed. Suddenly his quick ear informed him that some one was coming down the path towards the village. He heard the panting breath and the soft patter of the moccasins of a runner. Concealing himself, he waited the approach of the stranger. Peering from behind the friendly tree trunk, he beheld an Indian running down the path. Tecumseh knew in an instant that the runner was the bearer of an important message, for the young man was naked, save for his loin cloth and a light cape of deerskin thrown over his shoulders. On his back was his bow and quiver of arrows, and in his hand was a wampum belt and tomahawk. As the runner passed swiftly by, Tecumseh saw the war-paint on his face and the significant glint of red on the blade of the tomahawk. In an instant he realized, as the memory of old tales came back to him, that this was a messenger of war. With beating heart Tecumseh turned and ran back towards the village. He saw the warriors gather around the stranger, and after a few

22

TECUMSEH

Imaginary portrait, from "Tecumseh, a Drama,"
by Charles Mair

The Council Fire

moments' conversation, lead him to the guest house. Here soft skins were spread for his comfort, and he was served with food and drink. Meanwhile, the crier walked through the village, announcing that a council would be held in the evening to receive a message from Cornstalk, head chief of the Shawanoes, and the word flew swiftly through the wigwams. When in the early evening the great council fire was lighted by the wampum keeper in the space of open land between the river and the fort, the whole village had assembled. The chiefs and principal men of the village sat in an inner circle about the fire. Back of these in an outer circle were seated the warriors, and pressing close behind these were the women and children.

Passitotha, the old wampum keeper, gravely filled the curiously carved stone bowl of the ceremonial pipe with tobacco, and handed it to Puckeshinwau, the father of Tecumseh. Puckeshinwau, holding the pipe by the long stem festooned with coloured feathers, waited until the wampum keeper had plucked a brand from the fire, then blew a few whiffs into the air. Turning to the stranger, he handed to him the lighted pipe. After a few puffs the stranger gave the pipe to one of the lesser chiefs beside him, and thus the pipe passed from hand to hand, around the inner circle. When the pipe had come once more into the hand of the wampum keeper, there was silence broken only by the crackling of the fire and the lapping of the little waves along the banks of the river. Then the stranger arose, and lifting his right hand high above his head, thus spoke:

23

The Story of Tecumseh

"Greeting to the Piqua band of the Shawanoes. I am the voice of the Delawares, the Iowas and the Mingoes, and of Cornstalk, Chief Sachem of the Shawanoes, and leader of the Northern Confederacy. Did we not make peace with the Longknives (Americans) and bury the hatchet? Are not their white belts in the lodge of the keeper of wampum? But the Longknives are as the wind, which no man may bind, and as the water which slippeth out of the hand. Behold the red stream of blood which runs at our feet. It is the blood of our brethren, slain in time of peace by the Longknives of Virginia. This spring, Colonel Cresap, with a party of the Longknives, came into the lands which have been ours since this island (America) rose out of the sea, and which we have never ceded to the Americans. They hunted the game which the Master of Life had placed in our forests for the sustenance of his Indian children, and treacherously murdered the Indians whom they met. Later on, another party of the Virginians, led by one Greathouse, came into our country and visited a village of our people. Pretending to be friendly, they invited our people to their camp, and after making them drunk, slew them, men, women and children, so that none escaped, save one little girl. Thus were slain all the relatives of the great Mingo chief, Logan, the friend of the white man.

"But ye say, 'It is far off. What have we to do with it?' Have not ye, too, felt the hand of the Longknives? Have they not taken from you the lands which were yours of old, and slain your sons? They sweep over the land as the fire, and we fall as the trees of the forest. Band by

24

The Council Fire

band, tribe by tribe, will they destroy us, unless we so stand together that he that wrongeth one shall answer to all. Hearken, then, to the word of the great Cornstalk. I give you in the name of Cornstalk this bundle of five arrows. Each day let the wampum keeper draw an arrow from the bundle, and when but one arrow remains it is the time appointed for you to take the war-path. Gather then your braves and join the tribes at the Great Kanawha, and Cornstalk will lead you against the Longknives, and many scalps shall hang in your wigwams."

The address, only the gist of which has been given, was illustrated by the most dramatic action on the part of the orator, each feature, each limb, each muscle of the lithe body being pressed into service to make vivid the portrayal. At the opening of the address the braves sat stolid and impassive, the flickering firelight showing their powerful breasts painted in crude designs of various colours, robes of the bear or buffalo decorated with feathers of the hawk or eagle hanging loosely about their shoulders. As the power and fervour of the orator impressed his hearers, deep guttural exclamations were heard, but the decorum of the council forbade any further expression of the emotion which filled the assembled warriors.

At the conclusion of his address the speaker laid the war belt of black wampum and the bloody tomahawk at the feet of Puckeshinwau. For some minutes after the speaker had resumed his seat there was silence, according to custom, so that the orator might recall any part of his message which he had neglected to deliver. Then Maa-

25

The Story of Tecumseh

guaw, the Bear, one of the lesser chiefs, arose, and slowly gathering his robes about him strode into the arena and addressed the council. First, he assured the messenger that he was welcome to the village. Then, with apt and dramatic gesture, he pictured himself drawing from the runner's feet the thorns which had pierced them in the journey thither, washing his head and his body, and giving him food and drink that he might be refreshed. Then he condoled with him on the loss of his friends, wishing them an easy trail on their long journey to the happy hunting-grounds. Addressing himself to the Shawanoes, he reminded them of their pledges to the Confederacy, and called upon them to take up the hatchet at the word of the great Cornstalk, and prove that they were warriors and not squaws.

One speaker followed another, and the voice of all was for war. Those who wavered in their mind or were opposed to war were content to drift with the tide, and no oil was poured upon the tossing and turbulent sea of passion. Puckeshinwau sat silent and inscrutable, but no single detail of the scene escaped him. He, too, was for war. Fierce resentment of the wrongs inflicted on his race fired his breast. Ambition, too, lured him on. Was it not by his prowess in battle that he had raised himself to the chieftainship of his band? Cornstalk was growing old. Life was uncertain. Perhaps, the Master of Life had greater gifts in store. His mind leapt forward. He saw himself returning with the spoils of the victor, and hailed amid the rejoicings of the nation as Chief Sachem of the Shawanoes and leader of the Northern Confeder-

The Council Fire

acy. Putting aside the young Tecumseh who, eye and ear alert for every impression, lay at his feet, Puckeshinwau drew himself to his full height and waited with hands folded until all eyes turned towards him. His commanding figure, bearing the insignia of his rank, dominated the scene. Puckeshinwau began to speak slowly and quietly, and after a custom universally practised by Indian orators, in a parable:

"There is a bird of the forest which layeth her eggs in the nest of another. The foster-mother hatcheth the egg and feedeth and careth for the stranger as for her own, but the strange nestling, waxing strong, pusheth the other nestlings out of the nest to destruction. So it is, O, brothers, with the white men. When first they came to our land from across the great salt lake they were a feeble folk and few. Our fathers had compassion on them, clothed them when they were naked, and fed them when they were hungry. Our fathers called the white man brother, and whatsoever he asked of them they gave him freely. But now that the white men are so many in the land, they have forgotten the days of their weakness and the treaties which they made. They take from us our lands, they slay our brothers. We have been drawn into the quarrels between the whites, and have taken up the hatchet, some for the French, and some for the English, so that Indian has fought against Indian in a stranger's cause. We have been blind, but now our eyes are opened, and we see our pathway clearly. Take, then, this answer, my brother, to the chiefs of the Confederacy from the Piqua band of the Shawanoes. In five days we shall set

The Story of Tecumseh

out. There shall be none left in our village save only the old men, women and children."

Stooping, the chief took from the ground the belt of black wampum and the bloody war hatchet. Brandishing the tomahawk above his head, he began the war-song of his nation. Three hundred voices joined with him. The wild and terrible chant floated over river, plain and forest. Self-contained and impassive as the Indian is in his normal state, when he has once cast self-control aside, his wild and savage passions know no limit. Here and there in the circle some war-scarred veteran of a hundred battles sat undisturbed amid the clamour, gazing stolidly into the fire, weighing the consequences of war, remembering the bitterness of past defeats.

The council had now lost all semblance of order. The war-dance had begun, and the warriors who joined in it thereby signified that they had enlisted for the campaign. In a moment the faces of the warriors were streaked with the war-paint; tomahawk and scalping-knife gleamed in the firelight. All the incidents of battle were enacted with startling fidelity—the fatal stroke of the tomahawk, the *coup de grace,* and the twisting, circular sweep of the scalping-knife. The old warriors boasted of past exploits and the young braves of scalps yet to be taken.

Reluctantly the young Tecumseh accompanied his mother to the lodge. As he lay sleepless upon his couch, his brain on fire, the hot blood of his warrior forefathers pulsing madly through his veins, he could hear the war-songs, the whooping and shouting of the warriors, and insistent through all the clamour, the throb of the war-drums. 28

The Death of Puckeshinwau

CHAPTER IV.

THE DEATH OF PUCKESHINWAU.

THE next five days were very busy in the Shawanoe village. The young Tecumseh was delighted with the stir and bustle of the war preparations. He watched the old men making arrow-shafts and adjusting the flint arrow-heads and arrow feathers, and the women apportioning the rations of dried venison and corn. Some of the warriors owned flint-lock muskets. These were carefully overhauled, fresh bullets were cast and the powder-horns filled. From the medicine lodge sounded an almost continuous roll of drums, mingled with weird cries as of various animals; the medicine-men were making magic so that the war-party might be victorious. They came out and stalked through the village, wearing masks carved in grotesque resemblance to man or beast. Cheeseekau, the elder son of the chief, was to accompany Puckeshinwau, but Tecumseh was too young to go on the war-path. Preparations were finally completed, and the Piqua war-party set out from the village. The warriors were in high spirits. Each had his medicine bag or amulet to protect him from harm. Those who had dreamed the night before interpreted their dreams as most fortunate omens of success. The Shaman, or chief medicine-man, had assured Puckeshinwau that the gods were most propitious, and

The Story of Tecumseh

prophesied that the expedition would return in triumph, loaded with the spoils of the defeated enemy.

In their own territory the war-party made little attempt at concealment, but as they left behind them the familiar hunting-grounds, Puckeshinwau took greater precautions. The little army marched silently in Indian file, each warrior stepping in the footprints of his predecessor, so that no enemy might suspect from the appearance of the trail that more than a single warrior had passed. The wariest young men of the band were sent forward by the chief as scouts to spy out the land and to report any threatened danger. These scouts running ahead ascended any nearby eminence, from which they watched for smoke or observed the flight of birds or animals, which would indicate to the trained eye the presence of other bodies of men.

While Puckeshinwau was marching south to join the other tribes of the Confederacy of the Great Kanawha, another army was marching north towards the same point, the army of General Lewis, sent by Governor Dunmore of Virginia to punish the Mingoes (Iroquois) who had raided the Virginia settlements in retaliation for the unprovoked murder of the family of the Mingo chief, Logan.

General Lewis arrived at Point Pleasant about the end of September, 1774, with a force consisting of some twelve hundred men. Here he waited for Governor Dunmore, who had promised to join him with reinforcements as soon as the Assembly had adjourned. The Indian scouts had followed Lewis's advance, and reported to Cornstalk that the Virginians had gone into camp at Point Pleasant. The tribes of the Confederacy had responded to

The Death of Puckeshinwau

the call of Cornstalk. He now had under his command a force of about two thousand picked warriors all eager for battle. It was determined, therefore, to attack Lewis at once.

Point Pleasant was a long, narrow point of land lying between the Great Kanawha and the Ohio rivers. Cornstalk halted his forces a short distance from the enemy's camp, and constructed a breastwork of logs across the point from river to river. The Virginians were thus enclosed within a triangle, the Great Kanawha River forming one side, the Ohio River the other side and the fortifications occupied by a swarm of Indians making the base of the triangle. If the Virginians could not cut their way through the Indians, the only possible avenue for escape was by swimming the one or other of the rivers. But this line of retreat had been cut off by parties of Indians placed on the banks of both streams. No better plan of attack could be conceived, for in the event of an Indian victory not a man of the Virginian forces would have escaped.

Lewis remained ignorant of the proximity of the Indians and of the preparations made for his destruction until the forces of Cornstalk were within striking distance of his camp. He then despatched two regiments to the front under command of his brother, Colonel Lewis. The advancing parties soon met and a desperate engagement ensued. The Virginians, adopting the tactics of the enemy, fought from behind trees. The Indians attacked with such fury that the two regiments were compelled to fall back on the main body, having lost a num-

31

ber of men, including their commander, Colonel Lewis. General Lewis, on perceiving that the front line had been driven in, immediately advanced with his whole force and charged the enemy, driving them behind their breastworks. From these defences the Indians poured a deadly stream of bullets and arrows into the Virginian ranks. The voice of Cornstalk could be heard above the din of battle, urging his men in these words: "Be strong! Be strong!"

Repeated charges by the Virginians failed to dislodge the Indians. The position of Lewis was now desperate. He had lost more than half of his officers. His men were falling on every side. He was fighting for life like a rat in a trap and with apparently as little chance of escape. At this juncture, however, three companies of the whites, protected by the high bank of the river, made their way, unperceived by the Indians, to the rear of Cornstalk's position, where they vigorously attacked the Indians. The red men, not expecting attack from this quarter, concluded that reinforcements had arrived, and, losing heart, beat a retreat.

Lewis was left in possession of the field, but it was a dearly bought victory. Dead and wounded lay on every side. Puckeshinwau fell early in the battle in a hand-to-hand struggle, while leading his band against the first line of the Virginians. Before retreating, the Indians gathered together the bodies of their slain and threw them into the Ohio, and such was the burial of Puckeshinwau.

The Piqua band, much reduced in numbers, under the leadership of Cheeseekau, sadly retraced their steps to

The Death of Puckeshinwau

their village. The main body of the Indians retreated to Chilicothe, where a council was held. Standing before the war-post in the council house, Cornstalk asked: "What shall we do now? Shall we turn and fight? Shall we kill our squaws and children, and fight until we are killed ourselves?" All were silent. Cornstalk then turned, and, driving his tomahawk into the war-post, said: "Since you are not inclined to fight, I will go and make peace."

Governor Dunmore was then encamped within eight miles of Chilicothe. The representatives of the Indians made their way to his camp, where a treaty of peace was ratified. It was on this occasion that the Mingo chief, Logan, delivered his celebrated speech, addressed to Governor Dunmore:—

"I appeal to any white man to say if he ever entered Logan's camp hungry and he gave him not meat, if ever he came cold and naked and he clothed him not.

"During the course of the last long bloody war, Logan remained idle in his cabin, an advocate of peace. Such was my love for the whites that my countrymen pointed as they passed, and said, 'Logan is the friend of the white men.' I had even thought to have lived with you, but for the injuries of one man, Colonel Cresap, who the last spring, in cold blood and unprovoked, murdered all the relatives of Logan, not sparing even my women and children. There runs not a drop of the blood of Logan in the veins of any living creature. This called on me for revenge. I have sought it. I have killed many. I have fully glutted my vengeance. For my country I rejoice at

The Story of Tecumseh

the beams of peace. But do not harbour a thought that mine is the joy of fear. Logan never felt fear. He would not turn on his heel to save his life. Who is there to mourn for Logan? Not one."

Some years later, Logan, the friend of the white man, met the same fate which had overtaken his family, being murdered by dissolute whites while returning to his village from a trip to Detroit. The Great Sachem, Cornstalk, and his son, Ellinipsico, about the time of Logan's death were barbarously murdered by American soldiers while paying a friendly visit to the fort near Point Pleasant. News had arrived at the fort that a white man had been shot by Indians in the woods near by. The soldiers immediately raised the cry, "Kill the Indians in the fort." The officers endeavoured to restrain their men, but in vain. The bloodthirsty mob broke into the council chamber. The young Ellinipsico showed signs of perturbation, but Cornstalk, rising to his feet, folded his arms upon his breast and calmly awaited the fatal volley, saying to Ellinipsico, "My son, the Great Spirit has seen fit to decree that we should die together. It is his will. Let us submit."

SOUTH BLOCK HOUSE, BOIS BLANC ISLAND

The Burning of Piqua

CHAPTER V.

THE BURNING OF PIQUA.

AFTER the death of Puckeshinwau, Cheeseekau, Tecumseh's elder brother, became the head of the family. A very warm affection existed between the brothers. Cheeseekau was impressed with the character and ability shown by the boy, and spared no pains in his education. He took Tecumseh to the hunt, and taught him the use of firearms and how to throw the tomahawk. Tecumseh excelled in all boyish sports, and gave promise of becoming a mighty hunter. These, however, were but the pleasures of the moment; it was upon the great game of war that his mind was set. Cheeseekau had told him in minutest detail the story of the battle of Point Pleasant and of the fall of their father, Puckeshinwau. He had told, too, as much as he knew of the history of the tribes of the Confederacy and of their never-ending disputes with the Americans. The murder of Cornstalk and Logan, whom he regarded with a boy's hero worship, filled Tecumseh with hot anger and hatred of the white men. Now and then roving bands of strange Indians visited the village. Tecumseh studied with intense interest their dress, their speech, their habits, and eagerly questioned them about their history and the country in which they lived. All these things his memory stored

The Story of Tecumseh

away; unconsciously he was preparing himself for a career to which later on in life destiny called him.

Tecumseh had listened to many tales of war. He had lost a father in battle, and was now to see with his own eyes the horrors of border warfare. In 1780, Colonel Clarke, with a force of one thousand Kentuckians, made a descent on the Indian villages on the Ohio. Some roving bands of Indians had committed outrages in Kentucky, and the backwoodsmen, who hated all Indians like "pizen" (to whom, like a famous American commander of a later day, the only good Indians were dead Indians), were only too glad of an excuse to sack and burn such of the Indian villages as could be reached. It was quite immaterial whether the Indians whom the Kentuckians attacked had even heard of the occurrences for which they were made to suffer.

Colonel Clarke and his forces suddenly appeared before the village of Piqua. A few hours before the attack a Shawanoe hunter rushed into Piqua, bearing the news of the proximity of the Americans and of their evident intention to attack the village. Many of the warriors were absent at one of the summer camps. No one among the Indians had dreamed of an attack, as the Shawanoes were then at peace with the Americans. The force available for the defence of the village was less than half the normal fighting strength of the tribe. Runners were immediately sent out to warn the other villages and to ask for assistance in repelling the invading force. The women and children were sent into the woods for safety with such of their possessions as could be most easily trans-

The Burning of Piqua

ported. The Shawanoes, after closing the gates of the stockade, assembled in the fort and awaited the enemy.

Soon a flatboat containing a few soldiers was seen descending the river. The Indians greeted the Americans with hoots and yells of derision, as the boat, propelled by the heavy sweeps, made its way to the river bank opposite the fort. When, however, the enemy, undeterred by the fire of the Indians, which at that distance was productive of little effect, proceeded to set up a small field gun with its business-like muzzle pointing toward the fort, a good deal of commotion was visible amongst the garrison. The Indians stood much in dread of artillery, and even the bravest warriors would not face the "double balls."

The first shot boomed from the cannon, and hurtling through the air, crumpled a section of the stockade, which, rotten with age, fell like a pack of cards. At the same time a warrior, on the lookout from the landward side of the fort, called out that a body of Americans were advancing from the woods towards the fort. The Indians began to waver. Another shot from the battery fell into the fort, killing a number of Indians crowded in the narrow enclosure. Crying that they would not die like ground-hogs in a hole, the Indians swarmed over the defences and retreated towards the village out of reach of the shells. Once in the open, the courage of the Indians returned. Sheltering themselves behind the wigwams and the huts of the village, they opened a vigorous fire on the enemy advancing from the woods. The Kentuckians, accustomed to Indian warfare, advanced in

The Story of Tecumseh

open formation, taking advantage of whatever cover was afforded them.

The superiority in numbers, the more effective weapons and the better marksmanship of the Americans made the outcome of the engagement a foregone conclusion. Stubbornly the Indians fought on, slowly giving way before the advancing Kentuckians. This was Tecumseh's baptism of fire, though he took no active part in the battle. Overhead he heard the hiss of the bullets or near him the soft thud which told him that some bullet had found its mark. Wounded men singing their death songs passed him, slowly dragging themselves to the rear. Here and there lay the bodies of dead braves, the faces of some stern and composed in death, others with features contorted, grasping in clenched hands fragments of sod torn up in the death agony. The landscape, familiar since childhood, took on a strange and unwonted aspect. He moved as in a dream. Here and there, along the line of the American advance he saw, like twinkling points of fire, the glint of the sunlight on the polished rifle barrels of the concealed sharp-shooters. The keen, pungent smell of burnt powder filled his nostrils. A bluish haze of smoke hung in the woods. The crackling of the rifles assailed his ear, sharply punctuating the babel of battle, the shouting of the Americans and the whooping of the Indians.

The lodges of the village which had been passed by the Americans in their advance were already breaking into flame. The Shawanoes lost heart as they witnessed the destruction of their homes, and plunged into the

The Burning of Piqua

forest, intent only on escape. Clarke was too experienced in Indian warfare to permit his troops to follow the retreating Indians into the woods. He now sounded the recall, and assembled his forces in the village for the purpose of completing the work of destruction. Such of the lodges as had escaped were committed to the flames. The cultivated fields were harried and the growing crops and caches of corn were destroyed. The village of Piqua had disappeared from the face of the earth. As the young Tecumseh followed the broken remnant of his tribe into exile, he vowed, like the young Hannibal, eternal vengeance against the enemies of his race.

The Story of Tecumseh

CHAPTER VI

THE ATTACK ON THE FLATBOATS.

THE remnant of the Piqua band found refuge in one of the Shawanoe villages on the Ohio River. The Ohio was the great highway for trade between the Eastern States and the western frontier. Pittsburg, the Fort Du Quesne of Braddock's defeat, which stood at the juncture of the two rivers forming the Ohio, served as the eastern depot for this trade. North of the river lay the Indian territory, the country of the Shawanoes, Iowas and Mingoes, Wyandottes and Miamis. The country south of the river had been ceded to the Americans, but only a few isolated forts marked the American occupation. Here and there were scattered the houses of a few daring pioneers, the scouts of the great army of settlers who were soon to possess the land.

For the purposes of commerce the Ohio was navigated by flatboats, some of them over sixty feet in length. These scows were steered by a long oar fastened on a swivel at the stern, and propelled by sweeps, the swift current carrying them along with great rapidity. Large cargoes of goods for the trading posts and forts were thus carried into the interior. It was impossible to work back against the current, so the boats were broken up on the Mississippi, the return journey being made by the boatmen overland through the wilds of Tennessee

The Attack on the Flatboats

and Kentucky. These boats were often attacked by the Indians.

Having lost most of their possessions in the destruction of Piqua, some of the Shawanoe braves determined to attack the flatboats and thus make good their losses. Tecumseh, after much persuasion, obtained leave from Cheeseekau to join the expedition. The village where the Piqua band had found refuge was not situated on the Ohio River, but on a small tributary stream about three miles up from the larger river. The warriors, twenty-five in number, embarked in four boats which had been captured from the Americans in a former raid, and pulled down the stream to the Ohio. Crossing the river to the southern or American shore, they hid their boats behind the brush which overhung the banks. They then moved to a gully where the smoke of their fire could not be seen from the river, and there made camp for the night.

After the evening meal was finished, the warriors, wrapping their blankets about them, sat around the fire, smoking and telling tales. Tecumseh, feeling that he was no longer a boy, listened eagerly to these stories of battles long ago, determining that he, too, would leave a name which would live on the lips of his people. Presently the braves, having finished their pipes, one by one rolled themselves in their blankets and lay down around the fire. Wyeewaro, the Wolf, who was to take the first watch, sat erect, smoking his pipe and gazing into the embers. Tecumseh, excited by the anticipation of what the morrow would bring forth, was wide awake. He

41

The Story of Tecumseh

did not dare address the Wolf, but sat silent, hoping that the warrior would condescend to notice him.

Quiet descended on the camp, broken only by the night sounds of the wilderness, the weird laugh of the loon from the marshes, the shrill complaining cry of the night-hawk, and indistinct, yet insistent, the sense of far-away movement in the forest. Presently the Wolf rose, and, throwing his blanket from off his shoulders, replenished the fire. Seating himself once more, he turned his not unkindly face to the boy and for the first time addressed him.

"You are young, my son, to take the war-path!"

Tecumseh's pent-up feeling burst forth. He asked many questions of the old warrior concerning his experience in battle, and about the stories which had been told around the camp fire.

"Who, O Wyeewaro!" said he, "was the bravest man of whom you have ever heard?"

The old warrior gazed long into the fire before he answered. Then he said:

"I will tell you the story of the great Chief Biauswah. Returning one day from the hunt, he found his camp destroyed and his people dead and scalped. Following the trail of his enemies, he at last came to their village. He hid himself in the bushes. The shouts and songs of their feasting came to him. Presently his enemies came out from among the tepees, leading two captives, an old man and a youth, whom they prepared for torture. They first covered the old man with birch bark, and after lighting this made him run the gauntlet, beating him to

42

The Attack on the Flatboats

death with heavy clubs. The young lad was bound to a stake, and faggots were piled about his feet. Biauswah, peering from his hiding-place, saw for the first time the features of the boy, and lo, it was his own son! He loved the boy; so, not thinking of himself, he left his place of safety and stood before his enemies. He thus addressed them: 'My little son, whom you are about to burn with fire, has seen but few winters. His tender feet have never trodden the war-path. He has never injured you. The hairs of my head are white with many winters, and over the graves of my relatives I have hung many scalps which I have taken from the heads of your people. My death is worth something to you. Let me, therefore, take the place of my little son that he may return to his people.' His enemies were astonished, but they had long desired the death of Biauswah, so, releasing the boy, they bound Biauswah to the stake in his place. Thus died Biauswah."

Quietly rising to his feet, the Wolf walked over to a sleeper, and, bending, touched him on the shoulder. It was time for the new sentinel to take the watch. Tecumseh, fearing that his countenance would betray his emotion, turned, wrapped his blanket about him and lay down beside the fire.

With the first light of morning the camp was awake. The kettle, in which a savoury stew of venison and corn had been simmering during the night, was removed from the fire. The Indians gathered about the pot, dipping out the contents with their wooden spoons until they were satisfied. Then shouldering their muskets they walked

43

The Story of Tecumseh

up stream to a point about two hundred yards above the spot where the boats were concealed. At a word from the leader, one of the number climbed a tree which commanded an uninterrupted view of the river. The others concealed themselves in the thick underbrush which overhung the river bank.

The hours dragged on. The Indians, stretched at full length, patiently waited until the moment for action should arrive. Suddenly the sentinel appeared, half stooping as he ran towards them. With rapid and excited utterance he told them that he had sighted a flatboat coming round a bend in the river. It appeared to him that there were a number of men in the boat, though the distance was too great for him to count them. The half somnolent braves immediately awakened to life, relaxed muscles grew tense, deft fingers adjusted the gun flints, the pans of the muskets were liberally primed from the powder-horns, and the muskets advanced to cover through a rift in the bushes the face of the river.

The ambuscaders were ready. Tecumseh trembled. The beating of his heart sounded loudly in his ears. As he glanced down the polished barrel of his firearm, he saw that it pointed now towards the river and now towards the distant bank on the opposite shore. Yet he felt no fear, only a longing for the moment of action to arrive.

Meanwhile, the white men, little dreaming what a reception had been prepared for them, rapidly drew nearer. Their craft was not a single flatboat, as the sentry had supposed, but two boats lashed together, a

AMBUSCADE OF UNITED STATES FLAT-BOATS, OHIO
RIVER, BY THE SHAWANOE BRAVES

(Original painting by Fergus Kyle)

The Attack on the Flatboats

precaution often taken by the river men while going
through the Indian country. As the Indians had anticipated when preparing the ambuscade, the boats hugged
the American shore. The bateaux carried twenty men,
five of whom were passengers, the others being river men.
Bronzed by exposure to sun and wind, clothed in suits
of tanned buckskin cut into fringes at the seams, moccasined, their heads surmounted by coonskin caps with
the tails hanging down behind, these voyageurs might
well have been taken for Indians. Theirs was a wild
free life. The ever-varying panorama of the noble river
unfolded before them. Here the dark wall of the pri-
meval forest, there the rolling prairie, the feeding ground
of the buffalo and antelope, and at long intervals the
rough stockade of a frontier fort where, bringing news
of the outer world, they were ever welcome guests.
Danger, whether from lawless white men or from their
bitterest foe, the red men, dogged their path down the
river. This but added zest to life and fascination to the
great game they played.

So heavily loaded were the lashed flatboats that it was
impossible to work the sweeps. The crews, therefore,
with the exception of the two steersmen, lay at ease on
the bales, their rifles, never far from a woodsman's side,
lying within easy reach. They were reclining in this
position when the river swept them in front of the Indian
position. At a word from the Wolf twenty-five shots
blazed from the cover. The steersmen, erect at their oars,
provided an easy mark. Both were killed, and the boats,
unguided, swung broadside to the stream. Eight of the

The Story of Tecumseh

occupants of the boats were killed and several wounded. The Indians, immediately after the volley, threw down their now useless firearms, and ran crouching behind the cover towards the spot where their boats were concealed. The survivors in the flatboats, in the confusion of the surprise, fruitlessly emptied their rifles into the bushes. The Indian boats put out from the bank and pulled at utmost speed towards their prey. Tecumseh was in the bow of the foremost boat. A few scattering shots came from those on the flatboats who had been cool enough to reserve their fire until the enemy was in sight. One of the bullets splintered the gunwale of Tecumseh's boat and wounded one of the rowers in the boat next following. So complete was the surprise, however, and so rapid were the movements of the Indians, that the white men had no time to reload their weapons before the Shawanoes were upon them. Tecumseh's boat, coming on at full speed, struck the bateaux a glancing blow, sheering off into the current with oars broken on one side. Tecumseh, the rage of battle surging within him, sprang at the moment of impact, and, making good his footing, stood erect on one of the thwarts. Here, for a few moments he was hard pressed. Striking with the flat of his tomahawk so as to keep his weapon free, he laid three of the enemy at his feet before reinforcements came to him. The Shawanoes swarmed over the sides of the bateaux and soon put an end to the conflict.

The boats were pushed to the bank, the scalps taken and the dead bodies thrown into the river. Two of the

The Attack on the Flatboats

Indians were sent for the muskets which had been left at the place of ambush. The Shawanoes then worked the flatboats across the stream to the home river. In the joy of victory all tongues were loosed. Each warrior was eager to proclaim his prowess, but all conceded that the hero of the occasion was the young warrior, the son of Puckeshinwau. Having secured the flatboats within the shelter of the lesser stream, where they were safe from observation from the Ohio River, the impatient Shawanoes examined the prize. The bales contained cotton and woollen cloths and a number of excellent blankets. These, with barrels of sugar, flour and salt, constituted the bulk of the cargo. They discovered a quantity of powder and several chests of tea, and a miscellaneous collection of manufactured articles, such as would prove useful to the settlers in the West.

Turning over the cargo to appraise its value, the Indians discovered a young man wedged in the narrow space between two bales. He had been wounded in the shoulder, and had managed to crawl into his hiding-place, pulling some tarpaulins over him in the vain hope of escaping the keen eyes of the Indians. He was dragged from his retreat, and stood trembling with fear and weakness before his captors. Several of the Indians, lifting their tomahawks, rushed forward to despatch him, but the Wolf, sternly ordering them to stand back, announced that the prisoner would be taken to the village. Drawing his keen scalping-knife, the Wolf cut a lock of hair from the head of the captive. He then tore a couple

47

The Story of Tecumseh

of strips from a piece of coloured cotton, and tied bows in the hair of the American. By this ceremony the prisoner became the common property of the tribe, to be dealt with as the council should direct. The Indian boats were loaded with some of the lighter and more valuable articles of loot, and with their prisoner the Shawanoes set out for their village.

It was decided that the flatboats should be left where they were until the next day, the tired Indians not relishing the long hard pull against the current. When the village was at last sighted, the warriors set up the news cry, and the inhabitants, men, women and children, rushed down to the water. As the boats drew near the landing, question and answer were shouted across the water. Some of the more impetuous Indians rushed into the water up to their waists to assist at the disembarkation. Amid a clamour of voices the inquisitive Indians examined the spoils, and bestowed their cruel attentions upon the unfortunate prisoner. As he was led to one of the lodges, sticks and stones were thrown at him. The boys who followed the little procession took special delight in jabbing him with their spears. He was given some food and made secure for the night. A cord was passed around his body and fastened to a stake driven several feet into the ground. On the top of the stake a small bell was fixed so that the prisoner could not move without ringing it. His arms were bound behind his back, the cord being drawn tight enough to stop the circulation of blood. His hands were placed in a small leather bag, the mouth of

48

The Attack on the Flatboats

which was drawn close. He was then left to the long night of pain and terror. Meanwhile, the maiden warrior with the proofs of his valour (three bleeding scalps) dangling at his belt, proudly stalked through the village to his lodge, Cheeseekau at his side, listening eagerly to the story of how he had won his spurs.

The Story of Tecumseh

CHAPTER VII.

RUNNING THE GAUNTLET.

NEXT morning the squaws, gathering about the wigwam of the chief, demanded as their ancient right that the prisoner should be made to run the gauntlet. This was conceded them, and preparations were made for the cruel sport. In every Shawanoe village a tall post was planted firmly in the ground near the spot fixed for the council fire. This post was painted red in time of war. Arming themselves with sticks and stones, the women assembled at this point. Two of the braves formed the women in double rows extending from the war-post, and then took their position between the rows and close beside the post. The prisoner, naked, save for a loin cloth, was brought forth. At the far end of the rows he was given a push, and he began running down the long and narrow lane towards the post. The women and children, shouting and screaming, belaboured him with their clubs as he passed. His back was soon cut into ribbons. His unwounded arm was raised so as to shield his head. More than once he stumbled, when to fall meant certain death. His numbed brain held but one thought: he must reach the post of safety. The rows of cruel faces seemed to stretch before him in the never-ending horror of a nightmare; but at last, reeling as he ran, he reached the post and fell insensible at the feet of the guards. He was safe—spared, had he

Running the Gauntlet

but known it, for a fate even more cruel. Yells of rage went up from the women, unsatisfied in their lust for blood. Brandishing their clubs, they broke ranks and surged in upon the guards, who with difficulty held them back, until the unconscious victim could be carried back to his prison-house. Meanwhile, a council had been called to decide the fate of the prisoner. This was Tecumseh's first council, the first public recognition that he was no longer a boy but a man and a warrior. The braves sat in a ring and in perfect silence. Beside the chief sat the wampum keeper, a long smooth stick in his hand. It was his duty to record the votes for life or for death. This he did by cutting notches in the one side or the other of the stick. In the chief's hand was a war-club, which was passed around the circle. Those in favour of death pounded the club violently upon the ground; those who would give the prisoner his life passed it on in silence. As the club travelled around the circle it was evident that the captive was doomed. But few indeed of the warriors refrained from giving the downward stroke.

Tecumseh, who hated cruelty, and who was as magnanimous as he was brave, would have pleaded the cause of the prisoner, but the diffidence of youth held him back from committing so serious a breach of the decorum of the council. When at last the club had returned to the hand of the chief, the wampum keeper announced the verdict, which was death. The Indians, with the air of a holiday crowd, ran towards the lodge where the prisoner was held. He was presently brought forth, sup-

The Story of Tecumseh

ported by two braves. A belt of black wampum had been
thrown about his shoulders. His face had been painted
black and his head shaved; in his hand he carried a
rattle made of a dried bladder containing the toe bones
of a deer. The braves, who were gathered around him,
began a slow and solemn chant, after the manner of an
invocation, which changed to a quicker time, the prisoner
being forced to shake the rattle in unison. Thus the captive was led through the hooting and jeering crowd
towards an iron stake near which faggots were piled. It
was plain that death by fire awaited him. He was tied
to the stake, the dry wood was heaped about his feet and
the torch applied.

Tecumseh, who had never witnessed a burning, stood
at one side watching the proceedings in impotent rage.
At the first anguished cry of the victim, the young warrior felt as if the fire were gnawing at his own body.
His whole nature was outraged by the terrible spectacle.
Flinging himself on the guards, he endeavoured to force
his way through to the rescue of the prisoner, but in
vain. At last he was forced to desist. The vehemence
of his feelings found, however, another outlet. He turned
and addressed the crowd. Then was heard for the first
time the voice of the orator, matchless for eloquence
among his people, who, in days to come, was to sway the
councils of distant tribes and alien races. Like some
Hebrew prophet of old, he reproached his people sternly
yet tenderly, pleading with them to give up their barbarous practice, and denouncing the cruelty of their conduct which must call down upon them the displeasure

Running the Gauntlet

of the Master of Life. Such was the effect of his eloquence that the warriors, gathering about him, vowed
that never again would they torture a prisoner. The
promise was ever after faithfully observed. On the night
of the burning few slept in the Shawanoe village.
Tecumseh's fiery denunciation had stirred the people to
the heart. They felt that through him the Great Spirit
had manifested anger, and so all the night long they kept
beating on their wigwams to frighten the evil away.

The Story of Tecumseh

CHAPTER VIII.

THE LONG TRAIL.

THE Indians of North America were a people of a restless, roving disposition. The young braves, like the knights of mediæval Europe, journeyed forth in quest of adventure, sometimes singly, but more often in small companies under the leadership of some warrior who had achieved a reputation for strategy and daring. The ambition of every Indian was to become a war chief. In furtherance of this object he seized every opportunity which promised to add to his reputation as a warrior. Tecumseh felt this impulse to wander, to see strange peoples and to visit distant lands, growing day by day stronger within him. His imagination was fired by the stories told around the camp fires of the great wild lands of the West, the empire of the Indians, which the long arm and clutching fingers of the white man had touched, indeed, but had not yet grasped. He longed to float down the current of the " great Father of Waters," the majestic Mississippi, to see the vast prairies stretching ocean-like beyond the range of vision, and, perchance, to view afar the great mountains of the West which pierced the very clouds of heaven.

Cheeseekau was aware of Tecumseh's restless longing to see new skies, and resolved that this desire should be gratified. In accordance with the Indian custom, he gave

The Long Trail

a feast to which he invited a number of his friends, and after they had partaken of the rude dainties provided for them, he announced that he intended to form a party for an expedition to the West. He also told the assembled braves that he had gone into the forest, where, after fasting for some time, he had lain down to sleep. In his dreams the Great Spirit had made known to him that he approved of the plan for the journey, and had promised success to the venture. The medicine-men had been consulted, and after making magic, they, too, had assured him that the signs were propitious. Cheeseekau had already acquired among his people the reputation of a bold and sagacious leader. He, therefore, had no difficulty in choosing from amongst those who volunteered fifty young braves eager to set out on the westward trail.

Preparations were soon made and the journey begun. As the little company left behind them the familiar landmarks and pushed out into the unknown, Tecumseh's spirits rose. He felt the zest of adventure running like wine in his blood. Perils and dangers would beset them through the wilderness, accidents from field and flood, from the beasts of the forest, and from more dangerous enemies, their fellow-men. This was what they sought; adventures would come to the adventurous. For a time they camped on the Mississinewa River, in what is now north-eastern Indiana. Becoming restless, they turned once more to the westward, emerging from the forest on the banks of the Mississippi, several hundred miles north of the mouth of the Ohio. Here for some months they camped, fishing and hunting, exploring the country, and

The Story of Tecumseh

holding intercourse with the tribes of that region. Camp was again struck and they journeyed south along the great river, passing the mouth of the Ohio. On the journey south they encountered small and scattered herds of buffalo, the broken country through which they travelled lying on the verge of the great plains. The buffalo was not unknown to them, for small bands of these animals, following the narrow stretches of prairie which ran into the forest land, occasionally penetrated as far east as the Shawanoe villages.

At last they reached the prairies, and beheld in amazement the vast sweep of the plain, clad in the verdure of the sweet spring grass. They pitched their camp near one of the Mandan villages. Here the adventurers indulged in their first grand buffalo hunt. Though it was not "running season" (which is August and September), large numbers of buffalo could be observed feeding in scattered herds over the face of the prairie. Leaving their muskets in the village, armed only with bows, arrows and spears, the Shawanoes joined the Mandan hunters, mounted on tough, wiry ponies specially trained for the buffalo hunt. No bridle was used, a halter being twisted about the under jaw of the horse and looped over the neck. All superfluous clothing was dispensed with, in case the hunter should be thrown from his horse and have to depend on his fleetness of foot to escape the charge of the infuriated buffalo.

Having decided on the plan of attack, the hunters divided into two columns, and gradually surrounded the

56

The Long Trail

herd at the distance of about a mile. The circle of horse-men stationed at equal distances apart, on receiving a signal from the leader, gradually closed in. When the buffalo detected the scent of their enemy, they fled in confusion, but the horsemen meeting them as they tried to break the circle, by shouting and waving weapons in the air turned the rushing black mass in an opposite direction, where again it was turned back in a similar manner. The bewildered animals were now eddying about in a confused horde, surrounded by the close circle of the hunters. The work of death began. The Indians, galloping round their victims, drove their arrows and long lances into those they selected, aiming always at the heart. Clouds of dust arose, half obscuring the scene. Wounded bulls with bristling manes charged their pursuers, in many cases dismounting them. When hard-pressed the dismounted Indian snatched the buffalo robe from his waist and threw it over the horns and eyes of the infuriated beast, and jumping to one side drove the lance deep into the side of the buffalo as it thundered by. The well-trained pony, drawing out of the melee, patiently waited until his rider claimed him. The Indians did not desist from the slaughter until all the arrows had been shot away and they had their horses exhausted with their efforts.

Tecumseh, intoxicated with the excitement of the chase, rode in and out among the buffalo, selecting as his victims the largest and fattest bulls. Bumped and jostled by the running animals, he managed to keep his seat until,

The Story of Tecumseh

tired of the slaughter, he withdrew a little from the tumult of the carnage to rest his horse and to survey the scene. As he watched, he perceived a large bull which had broken from the herd running out on the prairie. Encouraging his tired pony, he resolved that the magnificent animal should become his quarry. Riding at full speed he was rapidly overtaking his prey, when the pony, putting his foot in a gopher hole, threw both himself and his rider heavily to the ground. Tecumseh was stunned by the fall. Fortunately for him, the accident had happened outside the circle of milling buffalo. On attempting to rise he discovered that his left leg was broken. Cheeseekau saw him on the ground and came to his assistance. The women and children had followed the hunters for the purpose of skinning the slain animals and cutting up the meat, and had with them a train of pack-horses upon which to load the spoils. Tecumseh was carried back to the village on a rude litter suspended between two of the pack-horses. This accident detained the Shawanoes for several months at the Mandan village. Tecumseh improved the time by mastering the language of his hosts, observing their customs, and listening to the stories of the past glories of the tribe, told by the garrulous old men who visited his wigwam.

After Tecumseh's recovery the little band once more pushed on to the south. When they reached the Cherokee country they found that tribe at war with the whites. The young Shawanoes were delighted with the prospect of battle, and needed but little persuasion to join the Chero-

The Long Trail

kees on the war-path. The Cherokees, elated by this unexpected reinforcement, resolved to attack a fort which the Americans had lately erected in their territory. The night before the assault took place, Cheeseekau, it is said, addressed his followers, predicting that he would be killed in the attack, but stating that if the Indians pressed on they would win the fort. The superstitious Indians endeavoured to persuade him to remain in camp, but he insisted on leading his Shawanoes into battle. As he had predicted, he fell. While being carried from the field he exulted with his last breath that he had received his death-wound in battle, saying that he did not desire to be buried at home like an old squaw, but preferred that the fowls of the air should pick his bones. Tecumseh, infuriated by the loss of his brother, attempted again and again to rally the Indians to the attack, but in vain. The superstition of the Indians had been aroused, they refused to fight any longer, and sullenly retreated to the Cherokee village.

Tecumseh now assumed the leadership of the wanderers. He told them that he was resolved not to return to his own country until he had done something worthy of being told. For two years longer the Shawanoes continued on their quest for adventure, reaching Florida, the country of the Chickasaws, Seminoles and Creeks, and mingling in the quarrels of these tribes with the Americans and Spanish. Many battles were fought, in which, owing to the skilful generalship of Tecumseh, the Indians were almost always successful. This was Tecumseh's

The Story of Tecumseh

first acquaintance with the southern tribes. He gained among them the reputation of being a brave and sagacious leader, which, when he returned later on his great mission, served him well. At last the little band, reduced to half its original number, turned homewards and reached the country of the Ohio in the fall of 1790 after an absence of three years.

The Dark and Bloody Ground

CHAPTER IX.

THE DARK AND BLOODY GROUND.

STIRRING events had happened in the Ohio Valley during the absence of Tecumseh. The smouldering fire of hatred between the Indians and the Americans had broken into open war. The causes of trouble were the same as those which had brought about the previous struggle. The average backwoodsman of Ohio, Tennessee or Kentucky hated the Indian with a contemptuous, yet deadly, hatred, and on the slightest pretext, or no pretext at all, shot him down like a wild beast. The Indian was looked upon as merely a cumberer of the ground, an obstacle to progress and an impediment to the opening up of the country. The flagrant injustice of the treatment of the Indians by the white men was, as Washington admitted, at the bottom of every Indian trouble. The white man's law, while rigorously applied against the Indian, afforded the red man no protection, either of person or property. By fraud or force the seizure of Indian lands by the whites went unceasingly on. Driven to desperation by public and private wrongs, the Indian fought his foe with the energy of despair. The atrocities of Indian warfare are indeed terrible. For torture and the stake no defence can be made, but the history of Canadian settlement proves that the inevitable displacement of the savage by the civilized race may take

The Story of Tecumseh

place without the horrors which have marked the extension of the American frontier, and which, for so many years, made the valley of the Ohio—the scene of our story —dark and bloody ground.

About a year before Tecumseh's return the Indians had defeated and nearly annihilated an American expedition led by General Harmer. In the fall of 1791, a second expedition under the command of General St. Clair penetrated the Indian country. Tecumseh, with a little party of Indian scouts, lay concealed near Nettle Creek, a small tributary of the Little Miami. From his ambush Tecumseh saw St. Clair's army on its march from Fort Jefferson to the north, and immediately sent word to Blue Jacket (Shawanoe) and Little Turtle (Miami), the principal war chiefs of the Indian Confederacy. Acting on this information, the Indians successfully ambushed the Americans, who were again defeated with great loss. The Indians filled the mouths of the slain with earth, a bitter satire on the land hunger of the Americans. The survivors, after suffering severe privations, found their way to Fort Jefferson, the ragged remnant of the army of the North-West.

For three years after St. Clair's defeat the Americans made no attempt to retrieve their laurels. A desultory warfare was still being waged between parties of whites and the Indians, but these were the usual skirmishes of the frontier, and cannot be dignified with the title of battles. In 1794, however, the authorities at Washington commissioned General Anthony Wayne ("Mad Anthony," as he was commonly called) to lead the campaign against

The Dark and Bloody Ground

the Indians. Wayne embarked with his army at Pittsburg, and floated down the Ohio in flatboats, landing in the Indian country near the mouth of the Wabash. On the site of the battlefield where St. Clair had been defeated, Wayne built an outpost, which he called "Fort Recovery."

Tecumseh, who had been following the American advance, resolved to attack the fort. This was a species of warfare to which the Indians were not accustomed. They never fought as a body, but purely as individuals. After the first shower of bullets all sense of order was lost; each Indian looked out for himself and fought as impulse moved him. These tactics were eminently fitted for the forest; indeed, the Indians were not finally subjugated until the Americans had learned to adopt their method of warfare, but the lack of a definite plan almost invariably rendered futile the attacks of the Indians on the outposts. The Indians with great bravery assaulted the fort again and again, notwithstanding a heavy artillery fire from which they suffered severely.

Perceiving that no impression was being made on the defences, Tecumseh reluctantly withdrew from before the fort, going into camp near by, so that he might observe the movements of the enemy. Wayne now decided to take the aggressive. Marching towards the Ohio so as to give the Indians the impression that he had decided to attack the Indian villages on the Miami, he swung round and by forced marches entered the heart of the Indian country, near the juncture of the Au Glaize with the Maumee of the Lakes. During their march the Ameri-

The Story of Tecumseh

cans were closely followed by bands of Indian scouts, but Wayne was not to be caught napping. Aware of the proximity of the Indians, "Mad Anthony" resolved to teach them a lesson. One night, having made camp, he ordered his men to cut logs about six feet in length. These logs were wrapped in blankets and disposed about the fire so as to resemble sleeping soldiers. The troops were then withdrawn a short distance behind a breastwork of fallen trees. The Indian scouts, thinking they had surprised a sleeping camp, rushed in and began tomahawking the logs. They soon found out their mistake when the Americans opened up a deadly fire from behind their defences.

Wayne in his despatches describes the bank of the Au Glaize as one continued village, so close together were the lodges of the Indians. The cornfields he pronounced to be the largest and finest he had ever seen. Far removed from the frontier, these villages had remained undisturbed amid all the turmoil, fire and bloodshed of the Border Wars. Having discovered that the Indian population was much larger than he had anticipated, Wayne abandoned the idea of an immediate attack, and set to work to build a fort. With the large force at his disposal this was soon accomplished, and "Fort Defiance," with blockhouses, magazines and barracks encircled by heavy palisades, reared its threatening front in the midst of the valley.

Little Turtle, the foremost chief of the Miamis, desired to make peace with the Americans, but Blue Jacket counselled war. Little Turtle, in addressing the council, said:

The Dark and Bloody Ground

"We have beaten the enemy twice under separate commanders; we cannot expect the same good fortune always to attend us. The Americans are now led by a chief who never sleeps; the night and the day are alike to him, and during all the time he has been marching upon our villages, notwithstanding the watchfulness of our young men, we have never been able to surprise him. Think well of it. There is something whispers me it would be well to listen to his offers of peace."

The council, however, decided to meet the enemy. The Indians took up a position at the rapids of the Maumee, behind fallen trees which had been levelled by a tornado. The battle which followed is known as the "Battle of the Fallen Timbers." Tecumseh led the Shawanoes, who occupied the forefront of the Indian line. He captured one of the American guns, but was forced to abandon it as the Indians retreated before the American advance. In the thick of the fight Tecumseh put a bullet in his rifle before pouring in the powder, thus rendering the firearm useless. Closely pursued by the enemy, his little band fell back until they came in touch with another detachment of his tribe. Snatching a fowling-piece from a wounded brave, Tecumseh fought on until again compelled to retire. As he fell back he tried to rally the Indians in a hopeless endeavour to turn the tide of victory; but the battle was already lost. The main body of the Indians had fled far into the forest.

The Indian villages now lay at the mercy of the conqueror. Soon ravaged fields and smoking ruins alone remained to mark the site of the Indian settlement in

The Story of Tecumseh

the garden land of the Au Glaize. This was a crushing defeat to the Confederacy. They had lost many warriors, and having suffered the destruction of the villages and their winter stores, starvation stared them in the face. Worst of all, the hated Longknives had established military outposts in the very heart of the Indian country. The fresh palisades and frowning guns of Fort Recovery, Fort Wayne and Fort Defiance dominated the land. By the Treaty of Greenville which followed, large tracts of Indian territory were ceded to the Americans. Although the Indians were held by the Americans to be firmly bound by the obligations of the treaty, they never received any of the benefits promised. Thereafter, General Wayne was called " Wabang " by the Indians, which signifies " To-morrow," in reference to his repeated promises that the treaty moneys would soon be distributed. Tecumseh refused to subscribe, and never recognized the treaty as binding upon the Indian tribes.

SHAUBENA

An Ottawa Indian and Warrior who fought under Tecumseh
at the Battle of the Thames, 1812

(From Nursey's "Legend of Pere Marquette")

The Open Door

CHAPTER X.

THE OPEN DOOR.

In early colonial days the French and English had agreed that the Ohio Valley should be regarded as neutral ground, the property of the Indians, but neither of the nations observed this agreement. From across the Alleghanies, from Maryland, Virginia and Kentucky came the English, and from the north and west came the French, both anxious to trade for the rich furs of the Ohio region. Outposts were established on the forbidden ground, and battles waged between the rivals. Instead of uniting against the invaders, the Indians allied themselves with the English or French, and indulged in a suicidal warfare, the only outcome of which would be the determination of the question whether English or French would be their masters. After the fall of Quebec and the cession of Canada, the English slowly drove the Indians back from every side.

As we have seen, the new Government after the Revolution pushed the frontier still further into the Indian country. The Indians by necessity were driven to form an alliance against the Americans, but the tie which bound them together was of the loosest description. In time of war some tribes refused to fight, because for the moment their own territory was not threatened. After defeat the Indians retreated to their villages, treating with

67

The Story of Tecumseh

the Americans by separate tribes and not as a confederation. From his childhood Tecumseh had heard the history of the dealings of his own tribe with the Americans. When he grew up he learned that the bitter experience of his own people was common to the other tribes. Steadily they were being driven from their ancient hunting-grounds. As the white population increased in number, the displacement of the Indians had become more rapid, and the land hunger of the Americans more insatiable. Divided into many tribes, some of which were the hereditary enemies of the others, quarrelling over the boundaries of hunting-grounds, involved in the petty jealousies of rival chiefs, the future looked dark, indeed, for the Indians of the Ohio Valley.

Tecumseh, as he witnessed the continually increasing pressure of the white settlers upon the territories of the Indians, began to ponder deeply upon the prospect confronting his people. He saw that if the Indians were to resist successfully the encroachment of the whites, they must unite as one body in a league under the leadership of the most distinguished war chiefs of the various tribes. The loose ties which since the days of Cornstalk had bound the Indians together in time of war, must give way to a permanent confederation, which would bind the tribes of the Ohio Valley firmly together in defence of the rights of one and all. The warriors must direct the policy of the Indians, not the village chiefs, who, even in time of peace, were ready for an entirely inadequate consideration to cede valuable lands to the Americans. Tecumseh held that the Indian lands belonged to all the tribes in common,

The Open Door

and that while an individual tribe had the right to occupy certain lands for its hunting-grounds, no tribe could sell these lands without the consent of all the tribes expressed in a general council. The council, representing all the tribes, would not, he believed, consent to a sale, unless it was to the advantage of all the Indian nations. In the past the Americans had not hesitated to conclude treaties of purchase with dissolute Indians who had no standing in their tribe, and having thus fraudulently obtained the cession of valuable lands, refused to give them up to the real owners.

Tecumseh determined to put an end to this robbery. This was the chief consideration which led him to form his Confederacy. He was anxious to avoid war, for he knew the inevitable result would be the cession of more territory to the Americans. If he succeeded in establishing the doctrine of the common ownership of the Indian lands, he would prevent improvident sales by a tribe or portion of a tribe, and thus remove the cause of many wars. Tecumseh's league would therefore be a guarantee of peace along the border, not a threat of continued hostility.

Laulewasikaw, the younger brother of Tecumseh, of whose early life little is known, now emerged from obscurity and began to play an important part in the drama. He assumed the role of a prophet as successor to "Change of Feathers," a celebrated Shawanoe medicine-man who had just died. Before announcing himself as a prophet, he had retired to the solitude of the woods, where, in meditation, fasting and prayer, he spent many days. After

69

The Story of Tecumseh

the custom of his people, he took a new name on assuming his office—Tenkswatawa—which means the "Open Door." In taking this name, the prophet signified to the people that it was through him deliverance would come. There is no question that Laulewasikaw assumed his new role under advice from Tecumseh, who desired to advance his cause by adding thereto the sanction of religion. Tenkswatawa believed firmly that he was a messenger from the Great Spirit, and began to preach his gospel to the Indians. It is said that before taking upon himself the role of a prophet he had been very intemperate. However this may be, he now led an exemplary life. The prophet was a man of commanding presence, but his features were not handsome and the loss of an eye gave him a sinister aspect. As an orator he is said to have rivalled Tecumseh, who was already celebrated for his oratorical powers.

Tecumseh's band of Shawanoes were now living at Tawa, in north-eastern Ohio. As the first step towards his dream of an Indian Confederacy, Tecumseh resolved to invite the tribes of the valley to a great council at Wapakonetta. The fame of Tecumseh and the Prophet had spread through the land, and a great company of Shawanoes, Wyandottes, Miamis, Delawares, Ottawas and Pottawatomies came to Wapakonetta to kindle the council fire. Solemnly the Indians seated themselves around the fire. In silence the ceremonial pipe passed from hand to hand. Then, after a long delay, the tall form of the Prophet emerged from the darkness, clothed in his robes of office, the black raven wings spread above his head. Amid the profoundest silence he made his way slowly

70

The Open Door

and with dignity to the centre of the circle, and, turning, addressed the warriors. He spoke to them of the days of old when game was plentiful and the rivers teemed with fish. "The Great Spirit had given the land to his red children for their hunting-grounds, but the white men coming from their own land were driving back the Indians. The Great Spirit was angry with the red men because they had adopted the bad habits of the whites. They must beware of drunkenness. In a vision he had seen the torment of drunkards in the hereafter, flames of fire issuing from their mouths; since then he had never tasted the firewater. The Great Spirit had never intended that they should live like the whites. They must return to the habits of their forefathers, dressing in skins and furs and eating the flesh of the deer and buffalo. They must make their bread of Indian corn and not of wheat. They must care for the aged and infirm and regard all Indians of every tribe as brothers. If they would gather together in one village he promised that the Great Spirit would give them his blessing."

When the speaker had taken his seat the question was debated by the assembly. Many of the chiefs, jealous of the ascendancy of Tecumseh and the Prophet, opposed the scheme; a large number, however, signified their willingness to accept the teaching of the Prophet. The new village was to be established near Greenville on the Maumee of the Lakes.

Thither went a great company of Indians of various tribes. Though Tecumseh was the real instigator of the movement, he preferred to remain in the background.

71

The Story of Tecumseh

The Prophet, therefore, appeared to be the leader of what to the Americans seemed a new religion. While the Prophet remained at the new village, preaching his gospel and welcoming the adherents who now began to flock in, Tecumseh was abroad through the valley urging the Indians to join the new confederacy. The converts rigorously practised the precepts of their new religion, and were peaceable and industrious. As the Prophet's prestige increased, however, he became vain and overbearing and made many enemies. He met the opposition by declaring that certain of his enemies were sorcerers, and by inflaming the superstition of the Indians caused the death of many innocent persons.

When Tecumseh returned from his mission he heard of these persecutions and sternly upbraided his brother. From this time forth he assumed the leadership of the new movement. Many of the Indians who had fled from the village under the cruel rule of Tenkswatawa now returned, bringing recruits with them. Nor did Tecumseh's journeys remain fruitless. Companies of Delawares, Miamis, and Wyandottes flocked to the new village. The stir and excitement among the Indians did not pass unnoticed by the Americans. The Governor of Ohio sent commissioners to Greenville to inquire into the matter. These commissioners were courteously received and a council summoned. Blue Jacket was the speaker for the Indians. He stated that he spoke for the Shawanoes, the Miamis, the Wyandottes and all the tribes of the Ohio Valley. They desired peace, and wished to live in harmony with the Americans. They had sent to their breth-

The Open Door

ren, asking them to unite in a band of perpetual brotherhood. Tenkswatawa told the commissioners that, in token of the good faith of the Indians, four of the principal chiefs would go to Chilicothe and see the Governor. Tecumseh, Blue Jacket, Roundhead and Panther accordingly accompanied the commissioners to Chilicothe.

Tecumseh stated to the Governor that the Indians had no intention of making war on the whites, that if war did take place it would be because of the aggression of the Americans. The league of the Indians was for the defence of their villages. He denied the validity of the Treaty of Greenville, which he said was signed by chiefs of no standing among the Indians. He protested against the purchase of large blocks of land from Indians who were not the real owners, and declared that the warriors had resolved that such transactions should no longer be tolerated. The Governor, being convinced that no danger was to be feared from the Indians, dismissed the militia which had been called into service.

Tecumseh's first plan, as we have seen, was to form an alliance of the Indians of the Ohio Valley for the purpose of holding the lands north of the Ohio River. He soon perceived, however, that even if he were successful in splitting the wave of immigration so that it would roll by him on either side, his territory would soon be but an island surrounded and cut off on all sides by the flood tide of American advance. He would then be exposed to invasion on every quarter, and could not hope, isolated as he would be from the Indian tribes outside the valley, to make a long resistance. His views so broadened that he began

73

The Story of Tecumseh

to think as a statesman, not as a Shawanoe, and a great plan dawned upon him. He resolved to form a great confederation of all the Indian tribes from Lake Superior to the Gulf of Mexico. The Mississippi formed a natural barrier to the west, the Ohio to the north, and he determined that the Americans should be held within these boundaries. The tribes along this frontier, strengthened by additions from more distant bands, should be wardens of the marches. Large villages might be established at intervals along the boundary and constant communication kept up along the line. A living wall would thus be opposed to the aggression of the whites. In pursuance of this plan, Tecumseh visited the tribes along the Great Lakes, penetrating, it is said, as far as the Red River of the north.

Impelled by the fire of patriotism which burned in his breast, Tecumseh performed almost superhuman labours. With one or two companions he travelled swiftly through the land, stopping at the Indian villages only long enough to impart his message, then taking again the weary trail or launching his canoe on the waters of unknown streams. He felt that the long day of Indian power was already drawing to its close. It behoved him, therefore, to redeem the time before the night set in. Wherever he went he was received gladly. Every tribe had its own tale of wrongs suffered from the whites, and eagerly grasped the promise of salvation which the plan of Tecumseh offered. His earnestness and the power of his eloquence swayed the hearts of his hearers. Like Peter the Hermit, he preached his new crusade, and the red men of the forest regarded

The Open Door

him as the voice of the Great Spirit, the man destined to be the Saviour of his people.

Messengers from the Prophet, too, had gone into the north country, two by two, carrying to the remotest tribes word of the new religion and the national movement. These messengers on arriving in a village announced that they were the representatives of a great Prophet who had arisen in the Ohio with a message for all the red men. With great solemnity they carried a figure, draped and covered from sight by rich cloths, to one of the lodges and there made medicine. The Indians of the village were admitted one by one into the wigwam. Here they were permitted to touch a string of beans, said to have been made by the Prophet out of his own flesh. This was called " shaking hands with the Prophet," and those who took part in the ceremony thus pledged themselves to obey his commands.

Tecumseh resolved as the first step in his plan to concentrate the northern tribes on the Ohio, as it was there the Americans pressed the Indians most closely. It was no part of his design to retake the lands which the Americans had already made their own. He hoped to save what was left of the Indian country, not to recover what was lost. He was not a dreamer, but a practical statesman. His plan was a noble one and offered the only hope of saving for the red man what was left of his inheritance.

The Story of Tecumseh

CHAPTER XI

WILLIAM HENRY HARRISON.

In the year 1801, General William Henry Harrison was appointed Governor of the newly-formed territory of Indiana, which embraced the country lying between the Ohio and the Wabash, extending westward to the Mississippi. The Indian lands ceded by the Treaty of Greenville were included in the new territory. Harrison was a Virginian by birth, and came of an old and distinguished family. He was about five years younger than Tecumseh, with whose story he now becomes so closely associated. As aide-de-camp to General Wayne, he had fought with distinction at the " Fallen Timbers," there for the first time crossing Tecumseh's path.

General Harrison was a man of great ability. As a soldier he showed himself to be brave, resourceful and energetic. Naturally, perhaps, he cherished great ambitions, and his actions were often determined by what he regarded as expedient rather than by what he knew to be right. His inclination was to deal fairly and honourably with Tecumseh and the Indians. He knew the wrongs they had suffered at the hands of the Americans. He admitted that " it was rarely the Indians obtained any satisfaction for the most unprovoked wrongs." In a letter to the Secretary of War, written during the first year of his

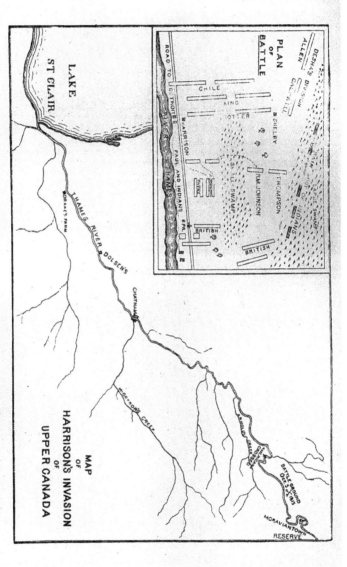

MAP OF THAT PART OF UPPER CANADA INVADED BY GENERAL HARRISON
AND PLAN OF BATTLE OF MORAVIANTOWN

William Henry Harrison

administration, Harrison said: " The patience of the Indians is astonishing, but if war should break out between the United States and any other nation, nine-tenths of the Indians would take up arms against the United States." These were his real sentiments, but the exigencies of politics led him to follow and, indeed, lead the mob of Indian haters and land-grabbers whose dearest wish would have been gratified if the Indian races had been exterminated. He bought large blocks of land from village chiefs whose right to sell was at least doubtful, knowing that he could depend on the arms of the United States to make good his title against the Indians, the real owners. In his messages and addresses to the Indians, following the example of all the American politicians of the period, he attributed the Indian troubles not to the real cause, the injustice of the Americans, but to the machinations of British agents. He told the Indians to listen to the voice of the Great Spirit through the Americans, and not to hearken to the devil speaking through the British agents. The Indians, on the other hand, complained that the British refused to assist them against the Americans. One of the chiefs graphically described the reception of the Indian war-parties at the British forts: " The English will not let us in, saying you are painted too much, my children."

In 1808, the number of Indians flocking to Greenville as a result of Tecumseh's labours was so great that Harrison wrote to the agent at Fort Wayne, asking for a report on the apparent intentions of Tecumseh. The Indian agent, after a careful investigation, reported that he could find no evidence of a hostile design against the United

The Story of Tecumseh

States, and thought that no danger was to be apprehended. The settlement of the Indians at Greenville had been opposed by the Americans when the village was first built, and pressure was continually brought to bear upon the Indians to leave the territory.

Tecumseh, having obtained a tract of land from the Pottawatomies and Kickapoos, at the junction of the Tippecanoe and Wabash, now moved with his followers to the new village which was afterwards called "the Prophet's Town." The migration of the Indians alarmed settlers in the vicinity, and reports were made to Harrison that the settlements were in danger.

Tenkswatawa, who had the most striking role in the new crusade, was believed by Harrison to be the leader of the new movement. He accordingly sent to the Prophet, asking him to come to Vincennes, the capital of the new territory of Indiana. Tenkswatawa sent a messenger to the Governor, accepting the invitation. This messenger, on being questioned by Harrison, said: "I have now listened to the Prophet for three years, and his advice has always been good. He tells us that we must pray to the Great Spirit, who made the world and everything in it. He tells us that no man could make the plants, the trees or the animals. He tells us not to lie, drink whiskey, or go to war, but to live soberly and peaceably with all men. He tells us to work and grow corn." On the appointed day the Prophet, accompanied by a small party of Indians, presented himself before the Governor. The Prophet, in his address to Harrison, assured him of the peaceable intentions of the Indians and explained the new movement.

78

William Henry Harrison

He asked that the sale of liquor to Indians be prohibited, as it was a deadly poison to them. Harrison secretly took some of the Prophet's followers to one side and offered them liquor, which they invariably refused. Governor Harrison, as a result of his inquiries, became satisfied that the Indians had no intention of attacking the settlements, and refused to move against them.

The Story of Tecumseh

CHAPTER XII.

THE COUNCIL AT OLD VINCENNES.

In 1810, General Harrison again sent commissioners to the Prophet's Town for the purpose of investigating the truth of rumours which had reached him that the Indians were preparing for war. The Governor of the territory and the Government at Washington were continually receiving petitions for troops to guard the settlements against attack which always threatened, but never descended. The consciousness of the wrongs they had committed against the Indians led the settlers to apprehend from the savages a sudden and fearful revenge. But the Indians had learned well the hard lesson that Wayne had taught them. All they desired was to hold for themselves and their children the rapidly diminishing lands left by their fathers.

The American ambassadors told Tecumseh that the warriors of Indiana and Kentucky were ready for war, but that they would act only on the defensive. Harrison's message was read in the council. In this address he said: " All the nations of the Indians united would not be able to resist the Seventeen Fires. Do not think that the red-coats can protect you—they are not able to protect themselves. They do not think of going to war with us; if they did, you would in a few moons see our flag wave over all the forts of Canada. What reason have

The Council at Old Vincennes

you to complain of the Seventeen Fires? Have they ever violated the treaties made with the red men? Have they ever taken anything from you?"

When this audacious message was read, Tecumseh indignantly made answer for the Indians. "The Great Spirit," said he, "gave this great island to his red children. He placed the white man on the other side of the Big Water. They were not contented with their own land, but came to take ours from us. They have driven us from the sea to the lakes. Now we can go no further. They have taken upon themselves to say, ' This tract belongs to the Miamis, and this to the Delawares,' and so on, but the Great Spirit meant it for the common property of all the Indians. The Americans must recognize this and give up the idea of making settlements to the north and west. I will go to Vincennes and speak with the Governor, who has been listening to bad men." The commissioners returned to Vincennes, and reported that they had not been able to detect any preparations for war, and that Tecumseh would come in person to see the Governor.

The meeting was arranged for the 12th of August. A few days before this date, Tecumseh set out from the Prophet's Town with four hundred braves in eighty canoes. The flotilla, glittering in the panoply of savage warfare, swept down the Wabash. At Fort Knox they stopped for a short time while Tecumseh and the commandant talked with each other. The blue-coats leaning over the stockade gazed in admiration at the warriors, the picked braves of the Indian villages. Tecumseh had no reason to be ashamed of his following, which well befitted a great chief.

The Story of Tecumseh

Launching once more into the swift current of the eager river, the party continued their journey. As they approached Vincennes the water boiled under the sure, strong strokes of their paddles, the canoes leaping forward as if endowed with life.

As the old fort, standing defiantly on the bluff, came into sight, a puff of smoke darted from the signal gun, followed a moment later by a dull report. It was evident that eager eyes had watched the river from the battlements. The population of the little town streamed down to the landing to see the Great Chief, of whom all had heard but whom few had ever seen. The canoes drew in towards the shore, but no brave left his seat. Presently, elbowing his way through the curious crowd, came the Governor's messenger to conduct the Indians to their camping ground, which was situated a short distance further down the river. When the Indians arrived at the camping ground, the canoes were drawn up on the bank and the wigwams pitched. Soon pots bubbled over the fire, sending forth savoury odours of boiled venison, and flat cakes of Indian corn were browning in the hot ashes. The Indians were at home in their new camp.

Vincennes was an old French town, founded in 1712 by Father Merunt as a mission station. The Governor's house, the largest in the town, was built in the spacious style of southern houses of the colonial period. Harrison resolved to receive Tecumseh under the colonnade. Seating himself on an elevated chair, surrounded by a group of judges and officers from the Fort, Harrison awaited Tecumseh. The Great Chief, accompanied by forty of his

The Council at Old Vincennes

warriors, approached until within a short distance of the portico, when he stopped. The Governor invited him to come in and be seated, but Tecumseh replied that he would not hold council in a house, but only under the open sky. The party then moved over to a grove near by. When the Governor was seated, he spoke to Tecumseh, saying: " Your Father requests you to take a chair." " My Father!" said the indignant Tecumseh, " The sun is my father and the earth is my mother, and on her bosom only will I repose." So saying, he seated himself Indian fashion on the ground.

It was a striking scene which presented itself to the onlookers. Around the Governor were grouped the officers of his staff and the judges and principal men of the town. Behind, standing at ease, was the guard, the bright August sunlight twinkling along the barrels of their rifles and on their polished side-arms. Overhead, lazily flapping and twisting in the light breeze of the summer afternoon, floated the Stars and Stripes, the hated emblem which was steadily forcing its way on and on into the Indian country. Once a sight to be told of by the adventurous Indian, seen in far travels to the eastward, now grown familiar, it floated over every outpost and stockade in the very heart of the Indian country. Seated on the ground, the centre of a circle of curious sightseers, silent, immovable, observing the decorum of the council, sat the red men. Proudly and defiantly they swept with their glittering eyes the circle of their enemies. They were warriors, not suppliants. The Great Spirit knew that their cause was just; in his hands was the issue. As for them, if need be, they would fight to the last to preserve their lands. Shawanoe, Wyandotte, Miami, Pottawatomie, Ottawa, Kickapoo and Winnebago—all were knit together in a brotherhood, the red against the white.

The great peace pipe of the Wyandottes, the elder brothers, passed slowly round the circle. The council was open. One of the chiefs was on his feet. He was beginning to speak. A whisper ran round the circle of spectators, who drew in more closely in their eagerness, for the orator was no village chief, but the head chief of all the tribes of the Ohio—nay more, the leader of all the red men, Tecumseh, the greatest Indian of his age.

Standing nearly six feet in his moccasins, erect, well proportioned and handsome, Tecumseh presented to the assembled Americans a splendid picture of aboriginal manhood. His frame, compact, athletic and muscular, indicated strength combined with great capacity for physical endurance. His head, surmounted by a bonnet of nodding eagle plumes, was of moderate size, his forehead full and high. His eyes, overhung with heavy arched brows, were black and penetrating. His nose was slightly aquiline, his teeth large and regular, his countenance was grave, almost severe, yet with an expression of nobility, courage and candour which never failed to impress the beholder. He was plainly clad in a suit of buckskin, fringed at the seams, and sparingly decorated with coloured quillwork. His only ornament was a silver medal, the gift of a British king to one of his ancestors.

Dispensing with the customary compliments, Tecumseh addressed himself directly to the Governor, speaking as he

The Council at Old Vincennes

always did on important occasions in the Shawanoe
tongue:

"Brother, I wish you to listen carefully, as I do not
think you understand what I so often have told you.
Brother, since the peace was made you have killed some
of the Shawanoes, the Winnebagos, the Delawares and the
Miamis, and have taken our lands. We cannot long remain at peace if you persist in doing these things. The
Indians have resolved to unite to preserve their lands, but
you try to prevent this by taking tribes aside and advising
them not to join the Confederacy. The United States has
set us an example by forming a union of their Fires. We
do not complain. Why, then, should you complain if the
Indians do the same thing among their tribes? You buy
lands from the village chiefs who have no right to sell.
If you continue to buy lands from these petty chiefs, there
will be trouble, and I cannot foretell the consequences. The
land belongs to all the Indians, and cannot be sold without
the consent of all. We intend to punish these village chiefs
who have been false to us. It is true I am a Shawanoe,
but I speak for all the Indians—Wyandottes, Miamis,
Delawares, Kickapoos, Ottawas, Pottawatomies, Winnebagos and Shawanoes, for the Indians of the Lakes and for
those whose hunting-grounds lie along the Mississippi,
even down to the salt sea. My forefathers were warriors.
Their son is a warrior. From them I take only my existence. From my tribe I take nothing. I am the maker
of my own fortune. Oh, could I but make the fortune of
my red people as great as I conceive when I commune with
the Great Spirit who rules the universe! The voice within

85

The Story of Tecumseh

me communing with past ages tells me that once, and not so long ago, there were no white men on this continent. It then belonged to the red men, who were placed there by the Great Spirit to enjoy it, both they and their children. Now our once happy people are miserable, driven back by the white men, who are never contented but always encroaching. The way, the only way, to check this evil is for the red men to unite in claiming a common and equal right in the land as it was at first, and should be yet, for it was the gift of the Great Spirit to us all, and therefore the few cannot cede it away forever. What! Sell a country! Why not sell the air, the clouds and the great sea, as well as the earth? Backward have the Americans driven us from the sea, and on towards the setting sun are we being forced, *nekatacushe katopolinto*—like a galloping horse— but now we will yield no further, but here make our stand. Brother, I wish you would take pity on the red people and do what I have requested. The Great Spirit has inspired me, and I speak nothing but the truth to you."

Having finished his speech, Tecumseh turned, and, walking back, flung himself down beside some of the lesser chiefs.

The excitement amongst the Indians was intense. General Harrison himself was so influenced by Tecumseh's eloquence that it was some time before he could collect his thoughts sufficiently to address the council. In his heart he knew that Tecumseh had spoken the truth. He could hardly bring his lips to frame the specious argument by which he hoped to create dissension amongst the Indians. He denied that the Indians were one nation. If

The Council at Old Vincennes

the Great Spirit had meant it so, he would not have put different tongues into their mouths, but would have taught them all to speak the same language. The Americans had bought lands from the Miamis, who were the owners, having lived there before the white men came to America. The Shawanoes had come from a distant country, and had no right to control the Miamis in the disposal of their property.

At this juncture, some of the officers surrounding the Governor suddenly drew their swords, and the guard, at the command of a flustered officer, levelled their rifles at the Indians. Seeing this hostile movement, the Indians sprang to their feet and surrounded Tecumseh. General Harrison, with the coolness of an experienced soldier, ordered the guard to ground their arms and asked for an explanation of the incident. He was told that while he was speaking, Tecumseh had denounced one of his statements as false, and said that the Indians had been cheated and imposed upon by Harrison and the Seventeen Fires. On hearing this, the Governor addressed Tecumseh with great indignation, calling him a bad man, and summarily dismissed the council.

Next day, time having cooled the Governor's passion, the council again convened. Tecumseh reiterated the determination of the Indians not to permit further encroachment upon their lands. He was followed by chiefs of the Wyandottes, Pottawatomies, Ottawas and Winnebagos, all of whom announced that they had joined Tecumseh's confederacy and would support him. Harrison then told the Indians that the Americans had good title to the disputed

The Story of Tecumseh

lands, and would defend that title with the sword, and
that Tecumseh's words would be reported to the President,
who would take means to enforce the sale.

The council then dispersed. Tecumseh and his warriors
returned to the Prophet's Town, while Harrison busied
himself with despatches to Washington, predicting a great
Indian rising and urgently requesting that aid be sent him.

BUST OF TECUMSEH

An imaginary portrait by Hamilton MacCarthy, sculptor.
Ottawa, 1896

Mutterings of the Storm

CHAPTER XIII.

MUTTERINGS OF THE STORM.

AT the beginning of the year 1811, affairs on the border appeared to be fast approaching a crisis. The settlers were determined to fight the Indians, and Harrison openly declared that the Confederacy must be broken. The authorities at Washington refused to sanction an attack on the Indians or to send troops into Indiana. With intent to provoke the Indians to hostilities and thus compel the Federal Government to intervene, the settlers, following their usual policy in such cases, inaugurated a series of attacks on Indians, a number of whom were murdered. Though well known, the murderers went unpunished.

A second meeting took place between Tecumseh and General Harrison at Vincennes. Harrison's speech was far from conciliatory. He demanded the surrender of two Pottawatomies, who, he claimed, had murdered white men. He refused to discuss the purchase of lands on the Wabash, declaring that he would put petticoats on his soldiers sooner than give up the land he had bought. Tecumseh replied that the Indians had shown a good example by forgiving the many injuries they had received at the hands of the whites. The measures he advocated meant peace on the border. He had no intention of going to war against the Seventeen Fires. The council of the Confederacy would consist of the ablest chiefs of the various tribes.

The Story of Tecumseh

With them the Americans could treat directly, and any agreement arrived at would be binding on all the red men. The Indians of the lakes had joined the Confederacy, and after this council he intended to visit the southern tribes, asking them to enter the league.

The council led to no better understanding between the Americans and the Indians. General Harrison gained this advantage, that he learned of Tecumseh's projected journey to the south, while Tecumseh did not suspect that Harrison was maturing his plans for an attack on the Prophet's Town.

Accompanied by a band of thirty warriors, several of whom were distinguished chiefs, Tecumseh, in August, 1811, set out for the south. " The party was mounted on spirited black ponies. The warriors all wore buckskin shirts, leggings, breech-clouts and moccasins. Both sides of their heads were closely shaven, there being left only a narrow ridge extending from the middle of the forehead over the pate down to the nape of the neck. The hair of this ridge was plaited in a long cue of three plaits hanging down between the shoulders, and the end of the cue was garnished with hawk feathers which dangled down the back. Across the forehead of each, extended round the head, was a band of red flannel about three inches wide. Semi-circular streaks of red war-paint were drawn under each eye, terminating outward on the cheekbone. A small red spot was painted on each temple, and a large round red spot on the centre of the breast. As the party proceeded on its way, messengers were sent ahead to announce the approach of the embassy. A council would be called, and

Mutterings of the Storm

the village notified would send out runners to gather in the tribesmen to meet and hear the great Tecumseh."

Tecumseh visited all the tribes along the Mississippi, and penetrated as far as Alabama, Texas and Florida. The Indians of the south, Choctaws, Cherokees, Creeks, and Seminoles, all signified their wish to join the Confederacy. To all these tribes he showed a belt upon which was pictured a disjointed snake, and below was the motto, "Join or die." In a speech to the Osages, which has come down to us, Tecumseh said:

"Brothers, we all belong to one family. We are all children of the Great Spirit. We walk in the same path, slake our thirst at the same spring, and now affairs of the greatest moment lead us to smoke the pipe around the same council fire. Brothers, we are friends. We must assist each other to bear our burdens. We are threatened with a great evil. Nothing but the destruction of all the red men will appease the Longknives. Brothers, the Longknives are not friends to the Indians. At first they asked only for land sufficient for a wigwam, now nothing will satisfy them but the whole of our hunting-grounds, from the rising to the setting sun. Brothers, my people wish for peace, but where the Longknives are there is no peace for them, except it is in the bosom of our mother (the earth). The white men have destroyed many nations of red men, because they were not united, because they were not friends to each other. Brothers, we must be united, we must fight each other's battles, and more than all we must love the Great Spirit."

Such was Tecumseh's appeal to all the southern tribes.

The Story of Tecumseh

At Tuckabatchee in Alabama, he addressed a council of the Creeks. His views were opposed by the principal chief, Big Warrior. Tecumseh, looking into the eyes of Big Warrior, said: " Your blood is white. You do not believe the Great Spirit has sent me. You shall know. I leave here directly, and shall go straight to Detroit. When I arrive there I shall stamp my foot, and shake down all the houses in Tuckabatchee." A few weeks after Tecumseh left, the famous earthquake of New Madrid occurred and demolished the houses in Tuckabatchee. The Indians, rushing into the open, declared that Tecumseh had arrived in Detroit. Meanwhile, Tecumseh had learned that it was the intention of the Americans to declare war against Great Britain in the near future. If such a war took place, Tecumseh determined that he would join the English, trusting that in the event of victory the Americans would be forced to recognize the Indian Confederacy, and submit to a delimitation of boundaries between American and Indian lands which would be guaranteed by the signatories to the treaty of peace.

Tippecanoe

CHAPTER XIV.

TIPPECANOE.

GOVERNOR HARRISON decided to strike such a blow in Tecumseh's absence as would shatter the Confederacy. He knew that Tenkswatawa, who was in charge at the Prophet's Town, was a dreamer, not a man of action, a religious fanatic, not a warrior. He determined, therefore, to seize this favourable chance of destroying the place. Tecumseh's followers, as yet only newly converted to the idea of the brotherhood of the red men, comprising warriors of many tribes, some of whom were the hereditary enemies of the others, would, he believed, lacking their great leader, fly apart on the impact of a superior force and scatter to their distant villages. In writing to the War Department at Washington, at this time, he said: "If it were not for the vicinity of the United States, Tecumseh would perhaps be the founder of an empire that would rival in glory Mexico or Peru. No difficulties deter him. For four years he has been in constant motion. You see him to-day on the Wabash, and in a short time hear of him on the shores of Lake Erie or Michigan, or on the banks of the Mississippi, and wherever he goes he makes an impression favourable to his purpose. He is now upon the last round to put a finishing stroke upon his work. I hope, however, before his return that that part of the work

The Story of Tecumseh

which he considers complete will be demolished, and its foundation rooted up."

Harrison knew that the Indians had no intention of attacking the settlements, but when he decided to move against the Prophet's Town, he trusted that he would be able to throw upon them the onus of having struck the first blow. So he again wrote the authorities at Washington, demanding troops for the defence of the settlements. Meetings were held at Vincennes and other towns, in which resolutions were passed calling on the Federal Government to take immediate steps to save the citizens of Ohio and Indiana from massacre. Messengers were sent into other States, asking for assistance against an Indian invasion. Governor Harrison himself went to Louisville, Kentucky, for the purpose of raising troops for his projected campaign. Governor Scott offered him every assistance, and before he left Kentucky he had received the promise that a large contingent would be sent. The President, however, had listened so long to prophecies of disaster which never took place, that for a time he turned a deaf ear to the cry from the western border, but at last permitting himself to be overborne by the clamour, he detached the Fourth Regiment under Colonel Boyd for service under the Governor of Indiana. At the same time he strongly impressed upon Harrison the desirability of maintaining peace.

The Kentucky volunteers arrived first at Vincennes, where Harrison was busy drilling the militia of Ohio and Indiana. The Fourth Regiment arrived some time afterwards, and the impatient Harrison, with a force of about twelve hundred men, immediately set out for the Prophet's

Tippecanoe

Town. He was aware that he was acting in disobedience to orders from Washington, but trusted in his star, believing that success would justify him in the eyes of the authorities. The Delaware spies had reported that the time was opportune. He resolved to seize the auspicious moment before it had passed, and to make good his threat of demolishing Tecumseh's work. But the General had been so eager to open the campaign that he had not taken time to collect sufficient supplies for the expedition, and was forced to halt on the Wabash while he sent back for provisions. Chafing at the delay, for his plan had been to reach the Prophet's Town by forced marches and to surprise the Indians, Harrison employed his men in building a stockade which would be a base for his operations in the Indian country. This outpost, which stood on the present site of the city of Terre Haute, was named in honour of the General, Fort Harrison. From Fort Harrison the General wrote to Governor Scott: "I am determined to disperse the Prophet's banditti before I return."

Supplies having arrived, Harrison left a small detachment for garrison duty, and set out once more with the main body of his army along the south-east shore of the Wabash. No Indians were encountered, and the Delaware spies reported that they could find no signs of their presence. The country through which the expedition travelled was densely wooded, affording excellent opportunities for Indian ambuscades. The country to the north-west of the Wabash was, however, more open, being indeed the outskirt of the prairie lands of the West. Reaching a ford, Harrison crossed the river, determining to take the northern trail, which, though longer, was safer and less adapted to Indian warfare.

It was not until the Americans had approached within three miles of the Prophet's Town that any Indians were seen. These galloped off towards the village, no doubt to report the presence of the invaders. The country here was very rough and broken, the trail leading through a deep ravine. Harrison was afraid of an ambuscade, and after changing the formation of his troops proceeded cautiously. He was aware that at this very spot the Indians had on two occasions waylaid the forces of Harmer and Clarke. No Indians were seen, however, and the Americans once more emerged on the plain. About two miles from the village, Harrison made his camp. Here he received a deputation of chiefs who came to inquire why the army had come into their country. They stated that the Prophet desired peace and wished for a council with the Americans.

Harrison promised to meet the Indians the next day. He told them he was ready to make peace, and with this assurance dismissed them from his camp. The officers and men were clamouring to be led against the town at once. They were "spoiling for a fight." Harrison, quite content to be persuaded, struck camp and gave orders to proceed. The Indian ambassadors had hardly reached their town with Harrison's reassuring message before the American troops were again in motion, marching in battle order towards the place. That Harrison made this movement, so threatening in appearance, with the deliberate intention of provoking an attack from the Indians cannot be doubted. He

Tippecanoe

had already made camp for the night. The statement which he afterwards made to the Indians, that he wished to find better camping-ground, was a mere subterfuge. Had the Indians been as eager for battle as the Americans, there is little doubt the conflict would have taken place there and then. Had the teaching of Tecumseh and Tenkswatawa been of such an incendiary nature as the Americans contended, nothing would have averted the clash of the opposing forces. But these Indians, pictured as bloodthirsty fiends, nightly dancing the war-dance, inflamed with hatred of the Americans, refused to pick up the gauntlet thrown down by Harrison, and without one hostile demonstration saw the American army, its front bristling with bayonets, march through the fields and upon the village. When, however, they saw that their town was surrounded on the landward side, and that the Americans were closing in by the river, they boldly ordered them to desist or it would not go well with them. Harrison then asked where he would camp, and was told, " Wherever he pleased, except within the confines of the village."

While this conversation was taking place, the officers and cavalry stood with drawn swords, and the infantry were drawn up in firing position. Harrison then withdrew about three hundred yards over a rise in the ground and made camp by a little stream. The Indians, in the meantime, had captured a negro found loitering in the town, and threatened him with death unless he informed them of Harrison's intentions. The negro told them that Harrison intended to deceive them, whereupon they let him go. Afterwards he came back to the village with a message

The Story of Tecumseh

from Harrison, telling the Indians to sleep sound and be at ease, that he would not allow any of his people to go near them.

The American forces settled themselves for the night in order of battle, the men sleeping on their arms. Triple lines of sentries were placed about the camp with guard companies at short distances apart. But in the Prophet's Town and in the camp, few found sleep on that momentous night. The darkness descended, black and impenetrable. Clouds covered the heavens, obscuring the friendly light of the stars. A cold, drizzling rain began to fall. The town lay in darkness save for the ruddy gleams of firelight reflected through the windows of the council house where the warriors were assembled. Outside, concealed in the tall autumn grass, the Indian sentinels watched the camp of the enemy, outlined by the long line of twinkling camp fires. At the guards' quarters the fires blazed high; dark figures moved incessantly across the lines of light, throwing gigantic and threatening shadows towards the Prophet's Town. Sharp and distinct came the challenge of the sentries as the officer of the day made his rounds of inspection. Harrison was not to be caught napping; skilled as he was in Indian warfare, he had made every disposition to guard against surprise. Let the bugles but sound the alarm, and in a moment, at the first notes, the camp would be astir with armed men, each going to his own place, alert and ready for action.

Again and again, during the night, American scouts crept up to the village. The Indians ordered the Americans to retire but did not do them any injury. Two young

Tippecanoe

Winnebago scouts were fired at by the Americans. Unhurt, the Winnebagoes dropped into the long grass and lay still. When two American sentinels came up to despatch them, they sprang to their feet and tomahawked the Americans. It was now four o'clock in the morning and many of the soldiers had arisen. Harrison was sitting before a camp fire, talking with his officers, when two shots were heard from the forward line of sentries. The alarm was sounded instantly, and the camp awoke. The firing had now become general along the whole front. The Indians replied vigorously. The warwhoop resounded from all sides; the battle of Tippecanoe had begun.

Harrison on his white horse rode backward and forward before his troops, encouraging his men. At the first alarm he had ordered the fires to be put out. Both armies, therefore, fought on in the thick darkness, the flashes of fire from the rifles alone marking the position of the combatants. The only Indians who took part in the engagement were the Winnebagoes and Kickapoos, and of these not more than two hundred fired a shot. The Americans were driven backward and forward between the two fires for about two hours. As the skies began to lighten in the east, the Indians withdrew, having exhausted their arrows and ammunition. The American loss was sixty-two killed and one hundred and twenty-two wounded. The Indians lost in killed twenty-five; the number wounded has not been ascertained. During the engagement the women and children crossed the river and thus made their escape. The Americans then moved forward and occupied the village. They set fire to the village huts, and destroyed the caches of corn belonging to the Shawanoes. The corn belonging to the Kickapoos was so carefully hidden that the Americans failed to discover it. All the trees in the orchards were girdled, and the brass kettles and firearms were broken and the fragments thrown into the fire. The Indians had driven away the few head of cattle which they possessed, but some hogs and fowls fell into the hands of the Americans.

The Prophet's Town, famous among all the Indian tribes, was now but a heap of smoking ruins. Harrison did not, however, long occupy the ground which he had won. After collecting his wounded and burying the dead he set out for Vincennes. The Indians dispersed, but later returned to their villages. Northward toward the Great Lakes and westward toward the Mississippi, small bands from the remoter tribes slowly and sadly made their way. Disheartened as the survivors were, they did not dream that with the disaster at Tippecanoe the last hope of successfully opposing the advance of the Americans had perished. A confederation of the Indian tribes was the only plan which promised success, but after Tippecanoe, even the genius of Tecumseh found it impossible to rally again the scattered tribes of the red men in defence of their common cause. That battle, insignificant as it appears, decided that thenceforth this continent should belong to the white man.

BARRACKS, FORT MALDEN (AMHERSTBURG)

Tecumseh Hears of Disaster

CHAPTER XV.

TECUMSEH HEARS OF DISASTER.

TECUMSEH set out on the return from his embassy to the South full of high hopes for the great design to which he had devoted his life, and which now seemed to be in a fair way towards fruition. His mission to the Southern States had been successful beyond his expectations. Such bands as had up to this time hesitated to approach, had now promised their adhesion, and the union of the Indian people seemed virtually accomplished. As the returning chief and his retinue neared the region of the Ohio, they were met by fugitives bearing the tidings of the crushing disaster which, in Tecumseh's absence, had overtaken the Prophet's Town—a disaster which, as Tecumseh from his knowledge of the inconstant Indian temperament instantly realized, was likely to prove a fatal blow to the great project. He hurried to the place which had been his home, to find his village destroyed, his confederacy shattered, and even his own band scattered among the different tribes.

It is significant of the courage and resourcefulness of the Indian leader that he wasted no time in bewailing the disaster, but set to work at once to do whatever might be done to relieve the desperate situation. He refused to accept defeat, but set out at once to visit the various Indian villages to which the members of his band had scattered,

The Story of Tecumseh

for the purpose of gathering his followers together. He was not, however, to be successful in his attempt at reconstruction. Strange as it may seem, his own tribe, the Shawanoes, had never, even in the days of his greatest power, given him a whole-hearted support. They now held aloof and rejected his proposal to found a new village. From the Delawares, who had long been the paid spies of the Longknives, nothing but active hostility was to be expected. The Miamis, Winnebagoes, Pottawatomies, Ottawas, and Kickapoos, when appealed to by Tecumseh, were friendly, but cautious. They desired to make peace with the Americans, and were afraid of compromising themselves if they openly lent their support to Tecumseh's schemes.

Brownstown (now Gibraltar), on the American shore of the Detroit River, nearly opposite Amherstburg, was the seat of the great council fire of the Wyandottes, the Elder Brothers of the Indian tribes. Roundhead, principal chief of the Wyandottes, was Sarstantzee, or head chief of the old Wyandotte confederacy. He decided to send messages to Tecumseh to inquire into the late trouble in the Ohio Valley. Colonel Matthew Elliott, of Amherstburg, Deputy Superintendent of Indian Affairs, under the British government, also sent a message by the Wyandottes urging Tecumseh to make peace with the Americans. A council was held at Mathethie on the Wabash. The Wyandottes, according to ancient custom, presided at the council. When they had delivered the messages of Roundhead and Colonel Elliott, Tecumseh rose and made answer as follows:

"Father and Brother Hurons (Wyandottes), you say you were employed by our Father (the King) and your

Tecumseh Hears of Disaster

own chiefs to come and have some conversation with us. We are happy to see you and to hear your own and our Father's speech. We heartily thank you for taking into consideration the condition of our poor women and children. We plainly see that you pity us by the concern you show for our welfare. We would deem ourselves much to blame if we did not listen to the council of our Father and our brothers, the Hurons. Father and brothers, we have not brought this misfortune on ourselves. We have done nothing wrong. When I left home to go to the Creek nation, I was stopped at Post Vincennes by the Americans, and was told that in spite of my repeated counsel to them to remain quiet and live at peace with the Longknives, some of the Pottawatomies had been making trouble. Of the truth of this I do not know, but I told the Longknives that when I came back I would make peace and quietness prevail. On my return I found my village reduced to ashes by the Longknives. Had I been at home and heard of the advance of the American troops towards our village, I should have gone to meet them and, shaking them by the hand, have asked the reason of their appearance in such hostile guise. Father and Brothers, you tell us to retreat or turn to one side should the Longknives again come against us. Had I been at home at the time of the late unfortunate affair I should have done so. Father and Brothers, we Shawanoes, Kickapoos and Winnebagoes hope that you will not find fault with us for having detained you so long here. We are glad to see you and to hear your own and our Father's words. It would surely be strange if we did not listen to our Father and our eldest

The Story of Tecumseh

Brothers. Father and Brothers, we will now in a few words declare to you our whole hearts. If we hear of the Longknives coming towards our villages to speak peace, we will receive them, but if you hear of any more of our people being hurt by them, or if they unprovokedly advance against us in a hostile manner, be assured we will defend ourselves like men. We defy any living creature to say that we ever advised any one, directly or indirectly, to make war on our white brothers.

"It has constantly been our misfortune to have our views misrepresented to our white brethren by pretended chiefs who have been in the habit of selling to the white people lands which did not belong to them. If we hear of any more of our people being killed, we will immediately send to all the nations on or towards the Mississippi, and all this island will rise as one man. Then, Father and Brothers, it will be impossible for you or either of you to restore peace between us and the Longknives."

As there were Delawares present, and it was known that they would report to the Americans all that occurred, the other chiefs were afraid to express their views and the council was closed, the Indians returning to their villages.

The Americans were already making preparations for war with Great Britain. Tecumseh had for some time known that war was threatened, and shortly after this council he saw that it was imminent, if not already declared. He resolved to join the British. His fortunes had reached their lowest ebb. The once proud and powerful chief could muster only thirty followers. But at the head of this little band he set off through the forest trails for Amherstburg to offer his services to his Father the King.

Tecumseh Joins the British

TECUMSEH JOINS THE BRITISH.

TECUMSEH proceeded on his journey to Amherstburg, gathering recruits in the Indian villages through which he passed. Governor Hull, of Michigan, a veteran of the Revolutionary War, had been appointed a Brigadier-General, and given command of the army of the North-West, which was to occupy Detroit as a base from which to invade Canada. He had arrived in Dayton, Ohio, to take over the command from Governor Meigs, and learning that Tecumseh was in the neighbourhood, sent a number of Wyandotte envoys to ask him to remain neutral in the approaching conflict. Tecumseh treated the envoys with great consideration, but told them plainly that neutrality was impossible. If the Big Knives prevailed in the war the encroachment of the Americans would go on unchecked, but if the British obtained the mastery, the rights of the Indians would be respected and full justice done. He pointed to what had been done by the British King for Brant and the Mohawks. Three times the Wyandotte Chief, Isadore, handed the peace pipe to Tecumseh. Each time Tecumseh broke it in pieces and cast the fragments upon the ground. " I have more confidence," said the Great Chief, " in the word of a Briton than in the word of a Big Knife."

The Wyandottes returned to Dayton to report to General

The Story of Tecumseh

Hull the failure of their mission. Tecumseh, however, resolved to visit Dayton and ascertain by his own observation what was going on in the enemy's camp. Arriving there at the end of May, he found the little town in a state of great excitement. Four regiments of the Ohio militia were already in camp. The Fourth United States Regiment, the heroes of Tippecanoe, were daily expected. Triumphal arches of evergreen, inscribed " Tippecanoe—Glory," stood in the streets. Flags were displayed in profusion, and the stirring call of the bugle rang out on every side. On the arrival of the heroes of Tippecanoe, the army of the North-West, twenty-five hundred strong, set out for Detroit. Tecumseh and his little band followed the army, though his presence was unknown to Hull.

The Governor proceeded leisurely on his way. War had not yet been declared, and he expected to be in Detroit before hostilities broke out. At intervals along the line of march the Americans erected blockhouses for the purpose of protecting their communications with the Ohio. The British held the command of the lake. Supplies could, therefore, only be sent overland, and it was of the utmost importance that this route should be protected.

Tecumseh, having ascertained the strength of Hull's forces and the route he intended to take to reach Detroit, left his Indians to follow the advance of the Americans, and hurried to Amherstburg to warn the British. This was not the first visit of Tecumseh to this historic town. He had attended the Great Council held yearly for the distribution of gifts and treaty money to the Indians. Thousands of red men flocked to these meetings, the great

Tecumseh Joins the British

majority coming from the United States. Under treaties made long before the Revolution, the American Indians were entitled to bounties, and Great Britain, with scrupulous regard to the pledges given, had continued the gifts, though the lands ceded had long passed out of her possession.

On his arrival at Amherstburg, Tecumseh presented himself before Colonel Matthew Elliott, Deputy Superintendent of Indian Affairs, with whom he was well acquainted, and formally offered his services to the King, the Great Father over the Seas. At the same time he gave Colonel Elliott full information respecting the American expedition under General Hull. Colonel Elliott asked Tecumseh to accompany him to the fort, where he introduced the Shawanoe chief to Colonel St. George, the officer in command. Colonel St. George was much interested in Tecumseh's narrative and kept him some time in conversation, taking notes for a despatch to Major-General Brock. It was decided that when the Indians arrived they should go into camp at Bois Blanc, an island in the river opposite the fort. Three blockhouses had recently been erected on the island, and the Indians, in case of attack, would be of great assistance to the little garrison. Tecumseh in the meantime sent messengers to the tribes in the vicinity, asking them to join him at Amherstburg.

On the 18th of June, 1812, after months of secret preparation, the United States of America formally declared war against Great Britain. The news reached Amherstburg about two weeks later. On the 2nd of July, the American schooner *Cuyahoga* was seen coming up the

The Story of Tecumseh

channel between Bois Blanc and the fort. As she was sailing past, a shot across her bows brought her to, and the *Hunter* moving out from the harbour brought her in as a prize. This schooner was found to be loaded with Hull's baggage, the hospital stores and intrenching tools, besides a quantity of ammunition. These supplies, procured at the expense of the enemy, were very welcome to the little garrison at Amherstburg. Valuable papers, including the muster roll of Hull's expedition and the general orders, came into the possession of the British.

Three days later Tecumseh's Indians joined him with the news that Hull had entered Detroit. The Indians then went into camp on Bois Blanc near the southern blockhouse. Shortly after Hull's arrival at Detroit, Roundhead, as Sarstantzee or principal chief of the old Wyandotte confederation, summoned Tecumseh to a council at Brownstown, opposite Amherstburg. By virtue of his office Roundhead had the right to call a council of the other tribes at any time. Tecumseh had ascertained that Roundhead, impressed with the strength of Hull's force as compared with the British, advised that the Indians should remain neutral in the war. This did not suit Tecumseh's plans, so he boldly made answer to Roundhead —" No! I have taken sides with the King, my Father, and I will suffer my bones to bleach upon this shore before I recross this stream to join in any council of neutrality." So great was his influence that Roundhead was forced to abandon the plan.

Hull invaded Canada on the 11th July, occupying the little town of Sandwich, which had no defences of any

Tecumseh Joins the British

kind. On the approach of the Americans, the handful of men who were garrisoned there retreated to Amherstburg. From Sandwich, Hull issued a grandiloquent proclamation to the inhabitants of Canada, in which he offered the Canadians "emancipation from tyranny and oppression and restoration to the dignified station of freemen."

He announced that "no white man found fighting by the side of an Indian will be taken prisoner, instant destruction will be his lot." "The first stroke of the tomahawk, the first attempt with the scalping-knife, will be the signal of one indiscriminate scene of desolation." Neither Hull's promises nor his threats, however, had any effect on the inhabitants of Canada. He expected that the Canadians would welcome him as a deliverer and would flock to his banner, but in this he was sorely disappointed.

Colonel St. George, aware of the weakness of Fort Amherstburg, determined that he would intercept the enemy before they reached it. For this purpose he established an outpost at the River Aux Canard, about four miles above Amherstburg. The river was unfordable, and there was only one bridge by which the Americans could cross. At this bridge he placed one company of the 41st, sixty militia and a few Indians. Shortly after the occupation by the British, Colonel Cass with two hundred and eighty Americans appeared in the vicinity. The bridge did not look inviting, so he followed up the stream in the vain search for a ford. The Indian scouts moved forward for the purpose of getting in touch with the enemy. They proved successful in their object, but were forced to retire, leaving one of their number dead. Thus the first blood

109

The Story of Tecumseh

shed in the defence of Canada was that of an Indian. Captain McCulloch, who had fired the fatal shot, scalped his victim, tearing off the bleeding scalp with his teeth. " The first attempt with the scalping-knife" was not made by an Indian, but by an officer under the general who a few days before had bitterly denounced the barbaric practice.

Again, though in his proclamation Hull had promised that the property of Canadians should be respected, he now sent Colonel Duncan McArthur of the First Ohio on a raid into the interior. This freebooter penetrated as far east as Moraviantown, robbing the settlers of provisions, blankets and cattle. On his return he visited Baldoon, near the present site of Wallaceburg, a settlement of sturdy Scotch Highlanders, founded a few years before by the Earl of Selkirk. The able-bodied men were all at the front, and as no resistance could be offered to the Americans, McArthur's troops confiscated grain and provisions. But the most severe blow to the colony was the loss of a flock of fine merino sheep which the Earl of Selkirk had imported from the Old Country. In recognition of his services, McArthur was given the command at Amherstburg, Hull being temporarily absent at Detroit. He determined to capture Amherstburg. On the 24th of July, he started out with a strong force to find a way of evading the outpost at the bridge. His scouts reported that a party of Indians had been seen between the Aux Canard and Turkey Creek, so he despatched Major Denny with one hundred and twenty militia to dislodge the Indians. Tecumseh, with only twenty-five Indians sent out from the British outpost as a scouting party, resolved to ambush

110

Tecumseh Joins the British

the Americans. When Major Denny walked into the trap it was sprung. On every side rose the Indians, shouting the war-cry and pouring a hot fire into the enemy's ranks. Panic-stricken, the militia broke and fled, pursued by their assailants. In their flight they threw away arms, accoutrements and haversacks. When the frightened mob burst through the ranks of the main body, McArthur became uneasy and decided to return to camp.

About the same time news of the capture of Mackinac reached Amherstburg. Lieutenant Hanks and his men, released on parole, had arrived at Detroit. Tecumseh, overjoyed at the news, sent his messengers north, south and west to the remoter tribes, announcing the fall of Mackinac and predicting the capture of Detroit. He called on the tribes to gather at Amherstburg and share in the spoils. He and his Indians constituted the intelligence corps of the little British army. Keenly observant, trained from childhood to discover the presence of an enemy while hiding all traces of his own, swift of foot, subsisting with ease where a white man would starve, the Indian was unsurpassed as a scout. Tecumseh despatched swift-moving bands of Indians to southern Michigan and northern Ohio, cutting Hull's lines of communication with Ohio, capturing despatches and intercepting supplies. Tecumseh had won over Roundhead, and the Indian camp at Bois Blanc received a large accession of Wyandottes. So dangerous had he become that General Hull suggested to Colonel Lucas of the Ohio militia and Captain Knaggs of the Michigan volunteers that they should disguise themselves and attempt the capture of Tecumseh. This, however, the officers flatly

The Story of Tecumseh

refused to do, stating that they would have nothing to do with such "foolishness."

Early in August, as Tecumseh lay at Brownstown with seventy warriors, he received word that his scouts had intercepted a supply party from Ohio, led by Captain Brush, at the River Raisin, thirty-six miles below Detroit. Brush had with him two hundred and thirty volunteers from Ohio as escort for a herd of one hundred beef cattle. Hull was expecting these supplies, and, suspecting by the delay that Brush was in trouble, he sent Major Van Horne with a party of over two hundred men to effect a juncture with Brush and escort him to Detroit. Tecumseh heard of the projected expedition and resolved to form an ambush. He had no time to send to Bois Blanc for reinforcements, so with his seventy Indians he took up a position in the thick woods on either side of the trail and awaited Van Horne. Like the panther from which he was named he lay in wait ready to spring upon his prey. The American force was mounted, and without suspecting danger rode directly into the ambuscade. At a signal from Tecumseh the Indians rose and opened a most destructive fire on the enemy, who, taken by surprise, wheeled about and sought safety in flight, pursued by the Indians. Tecumseh lost only one man in this skirmish, while the loss of the Americans was eighteen killed, twelve wounded and seventy missing.

Important despatches fell into Tecumseh's hands as a result of the victory. These he at once transmitted to Colonel Procter, who had taken over the command at Amherstburg. From the captured letters it appeared that

112

Tecumseh Joins the British

there was a great deal of dissension among the officers in Detroit. The General had lost the confidence of his subordinates, and a party in the garrison was in favour of supplanting him in the command. When Van Horne arrived in Detroit with the shattered remnant of his command, Hull was seriously alarmed and immediately withdrew his forces from Canada, with the exception of a small detachment under Major Denny. To Tecumseh, therefore, belongs the credit of forcing Hull to abandon his offensive campaign and concentrate his forces for the defence of Detroit.

Hull saw that it was of vital importance that he should reopen communications with the Ohio. He, therefore, ordered Colonel Miller of the Fourth United States Regiment, with a force of seven hundred men—cavalry, infantry and artillery—to hold himself in readiness to proceed to the Raisin, and decided to send couriers to Brush, announcing the despatch of the relief expedition. Two days before the date fixed for Miller's departure from Detroit, as evening fell three of Hull's men, disguised as Indians, their hair and faces stained copper colour with walnut juice, stole out from the little town. Their plan was to make a detour through the forest, emerging on the Ohio trail some distance below Brownstown. It was thought that they could there obtain horses from the settlers and so push on rapidly towards the Raisin. Skilled woodsmen as they were, they lost their way, nevertheless, in the dark forest. Miscalculating the distance which they had covered and thinking that Brownstown was already passed, they struck eastward towards the river road. They felt that they

The Story of Tecumseh

had eluded the vigilance of the Indian scouts, and their spirits rose as they proceeded cautiously through the woods at the edge of the trail. Suddenly, without sound or warning, an Indian brave stepped from behind a tree trunk and stood before them, his uplifted tomahawk in his hand. For a moment the disguised white men stood silent, immovable, regarding with uncomprehending eyes the threatening figure which blocked the path. Had imagination played them false once more, as had so often happened in the long dark hours since they had left the fort? They were not long in doubt. Three times in quick succession there issued from the lips of the warrior the hoot of an owl. From the woods on either side of the trail came answering cries as the Indian scouts, converging towards their leader, surrounded the Americans. Torches of birch bark were lighted, and, holding these above their heads, the Indians peered into the faces of their captives. The flickering light of the torches showed the Americans a circle of Indians shining in war-paint, armed with tomahawk, rifle and scalping-knife. The suspicions of the Indians were verified. Their keen eyes soon penetrated the disguise, indeed the terror so plainly manifested by the Americans was alone sufficient to have betrayed them. At a word from the leader the prisoners were seized and disarmed. The papers in their possession were taken by the chief and deposited in a leather bag which hung from his belt. Each captive was placed between two Indians, his arms being firmly bound to his guards by buckskin thongs. The party then proceeded along the trail southward toward Brownstown, where Tecumseh had established his quarters. On

Tecumseh Joins the British

reaching the Indian camp the prisoners were immediately brought before Tecumseh. The chief sat on a pile of furs in his wigwam, surrounded by his bodyguard. He listened to the report of his scouts, and afterwards examined the captured despatches. As he read, the unfortunate prisoners gazed on the sphinx-like countenance of the chief, eager to decipher his intentions concerning them. Courageous and daring as these men were, inured to the hardships and dangers of life on the frontier, the prospect of torture and death unnerved them. The suspense was almost beyond their strength. Presently Tecumseh looked up, and, perceiving the mute appeal for mercy in the eyes of the prisoners, spoke kindly to them. "Fear nothing, you shall be sent as prisoners to Amherstburg." Turning to his brother-in-law, Wasegoboah, Tecumseh gave him the captured despatches, and ordered him to take the prisoners under escort to Amherstburg, and there deliver them to Colonel Procter. The next day Major Muir with one hundred men of the Forty-first Regiment and sixty militia arrived at Brownstown, having been sent by Procter in response to Tecumseh's appeal for reinforcements. Seventy Chippewas under Caldwell arrived in camp on the same day, making the total Indian force about two hundred warriors.

Early in the morning of Sunday, the 9th of August, the British camp was awakened by the distant call of the Indian scouts, who soon came running through the woods shouting the news cry. They brought word that the Americans were advancing on the British position, and were then about eight miles distant. Muir, after consultation with Tecumseh, resolved to meet the Americans at Magagua, an Indian village about three miles north of

The Story of Tecumseh

Brownstown. The British force was soon under way, marching down the muddy road which wound through a dark and gloomy forest. The scene was a striking one. Overhead the thick branches met across the road, making a twilight in the woods through which, a thread of scarlet, gleamed the uniforms of the regulars. On either side the Indians, their faces and almost naked bodies shining with war-paint, glided silently by, intent only on reaching the enemy unperceived. Armed to the teeth with rifles, toma-hawks, war clubs, spears, bows and arrows and scalping-knives, they might well strike terror to the hearts of the enemy. As the little force advanced it passed the scene of Van Horne's defeat. The bodies of the slain lay where they had fallen, men and horses " in one red burial blent." Disturbed by the approach of the little army, lean grey wolves stole noiselessly into the forest, and ravens hoarsely croaking flew heavily away.

The noisome odour of death and decay was heavy on the morning air, overpowering the sweet perfume of the summer woods. About a quarter of a mile beyond Maga-gua the command halted. Tecumseh and his Indians occu-pied the woods to the left of the road, and Muir deployed to the right, where he constructed a breastwork of logs and fallen trees. Having made these dispositions, the little army awaited the enemy. Soon a shot echoed through the woods, followed by the warwhoops of the Indians and the sound of heavy firing. The left wing was engaged with the enemy. After the first volley the Lake Indians turned and fled. Immediately after the right wing was attacked. The American force, consisting of riflemen of Ohio and Kentucky, were accustomed to border warfare.

Tecumseh Joins the British

Their uniform of rough grey homespun was inconspicuous in the woods, and taking cover behind the tree trunks, they fired into the British ranks, whose position was disclosed by the glaring scarlet of the uniforms. The American artillery placed in the road hurled shot and shell against the frail breastworks. Major Muir was twice wounded, and Tecumseh was hit by a buckshot. An unfortunate mistake added to their difficulties. A body of Indians at the rear of Muir's position was mistaken for a corps of the enemy, and a brisk fire was opened upon them which they returned with interest. Attacked apparently from all sides by an overwhelming force, Muir, who lay on a stretcher, gave the order to retreat. The British gave way, falling back towards the river, where without further molestation from the enemy they joined the boats and returned to Amherstburg.

Miller did not dare continue his march, but retreated towards Detroit, closely followed by the Indians. Lieutenant Rolette, the energetic commander of the *Hunter,* captured several boats loaded with ammunition which had followed the American advance by way of the river. The British loss in the engagement was six killed and twenty-one wounded. The Indians lost about forty killed, the number of wounded not being ascertained. The loss of the Americans was eighteen killed and fifty-seven wounded. Though the Americans had forced the British from the ground, they abandoned the object which they had set out to accomplish, and sought refuge within the walls of Detroit. Immediately afterward Hull withdrew Denny's detachment from Sandwich. The soil of Canada was once more free from the foot of the invader.

The Story of Tecumseh

CHAPTER XVII.

BROCK AND TECUMSEH MEET.

ON the 13th of August, 1812, His Majesty's Ship *General Hunter* lay at anchor in the Detroit river below Amherstburg. The day was bright and clear. Up the blue expanse of the river, Bois Blanc Island could be seen embosomed in the divided waters of the placid stream, the white walls of the new blockhouse and the wigwams of the Indians standing out clearly and distinctly against the green background of the forest. To the southward the noble river, gradually widening, lost itself in the expanse of the lake. All day long the officers and men impatiently scanned the river's face, endeavouring, in vain, to pierce the glimmering haze which hung over the entrance to the lake. The sunset gun reverberated from Fort Amherstburg. Twilight fell. Over the dark forest on the eastern shore shone a glory of silver light, as the full August moon climbed up the sky and flooded land and river with radiance. As the hours sped on, all the crew of the *General Hunter* save the watch retired. Lieutenant Rolette, officer of the watch, after glancing at his timepiece, ordered a sailor to sound eight bells (midnight), the signal for the change of watch. Before leaving the deck the lieutenant walked to the stern, and, leaning on the rail, gazed down the river. The silence of night brooded over the scene, broken only by the rippling of the

118

current against the sides of the schooner. The thoughts of the young man went back to his childhood home in French Canada, situated on the shore of the mighty St. Lawrence. In imagination he saw again the old familiar landscape, the white cottages clustered about the parish church, from whose tall spire descended the sweet familiar notes of the " Angelus " in evening blessing upon the land. But another sound broke in upon his reverie. His trained ear detected the creaking of oarlocks. In a moment he was alert, and, calling the officer of the watch to his side, he listened intently to the significant sound. Soon there was no doubt in the mind of either, for the noise of oars moving in the rowlocks and the splash of blades in the water could be plainly heard. Boats were moving up the river, and indeed could now be perceived, dim moving shapes faintly outlined against the blackness of the Canadian shore. One of the men of the watch tumbled below with orders for all hands to come on deck while the officer of the watch sent his challenge across the water, "Who goes there ?"

Clear and distinct came the answer, " A friend; who are you ?"

" His Majesty's Ship *General Hunter;* who are you ?"

"His Excellency Major-General Brock with reinforcements for Amherstburg."

A ringing cheer went up from the sailors gathered at the rail. On the *Hunter* guns were run out, and as the little flotilla passed, their iron voices rang out in a salute to the commander of His Majesty's forces in Upper Canada. Lights twinkled on Bois Blanc, and as the boats

The Story of Tecumseh

rounded in to the landing at Amherstburg, the Indians gathered at the water's edge, greeted the General with shouting, singing and the discharge of firearms. At the little wharf Colonel Procter, Colonel Elliott and the officers of the garrison awaited the General. As Brock walked up from the river he called Colonel Elliott's attention to the firing on Bois Blanc, and asked him to request the Indians to refrain from such useless waste of ammunition.

Although it was now past midnight, Brock, with that energy which always characterized him, summoned a council of war to meet in an hour in Colonel Elliott's quarters. Meanwhile he read the despatches and correspondence captured by Tecumseh at Magagua and Brownstown, and listened to Colonel Elliott's explanation of the position of affairs in the West. In the busy brain of the commander, the plan of campaign to be laid before the council shaped itself, clear and definite in every detail. As the hour appointed for the council drew near, Colonel Elliott, closely followed by four Indians, entered the room where the General was at work at a table littered with plans, maps, despatches and papers of every description. The apartment in which the General sat was lighted by tallow candles placed in sconces about the walls. Two high brass candlesticks stood on the table, the yellow flame from the candles flickering in the draft from the open window. The General, immersed in his work, did not look up. The only sound which broke the silence was the ticking of a clock on the mantel and the scratching of the quill racing over the paper. Presently he raised his head, and saw before him, as he expected, Colonel Elliott.

120

Brock and Tecumseh Meet

But the Colonel was not alone. Beside him stood another and more imposing figure, that of Tecumseh, clad as was the custom of the chief in a plain suit of tanned buckskin. A silver-mounted tomahawk and a knife in a leather case hung from his belt. He moved with a dignity, a distinction of manner which marked him as a born leader of men. Brock rose to his feet as Colonel Elliott addressed him: " This, sir, is the celebrated Chief Tecumseh of whom you have heard, and who desires to be presented to you." The General advanced with outstretched hand to greet his great ally. Tecumseh swept with lightning glance the gallant figure approaching, and recognized a spirit as lofty as his own. Tall and stalwart, fair-haired and blue-eyed, Brock was an example of the best type of British officer. Their hands met in a firm clasp, typical of that alliance between red men and white which, by the grace of God, was to prove the salvation of Canada in this her hour of peril. Brock and Tecumseh gazed into each other's eyes, and knew that their souls were akin. Each recognized that

> " There is neither East nor West,
>   Border nor breed nor birth,
> When two strong men stand face to face,
>   Though they come from the ends of the earth."

Turning to his followers, Tecumseh exclaimed, "This is a man!" The attendant chiefs assented in emphatic " Ughs " and " Ho-hos."

"In the name of the Great Father over the sea," said Brock, " I thank Tecumseh and his braves for the great services they have rendered the British in this war. They

The Story of Tecumseh

have been the eyes and the ears of our little army of the West. I have read the despatches which our Indian allies captured from the Longknives at Brownstown and Magagua, and at other times, and upon the information therein contained I intend to act."

While Brock was speaking, the officers who were to compose the council began to assemble. Colonels Procter, St. George and Elliott, Quartermaster-General Nichol, Majors Chambers, Tallon, Glegg and Givins and Captain Dixon of the Royal Artillery drew their chairs to the table. Brock placed Tecumseh at his right; at his left sat the gallant Macdonell, who had thrown aside the silken robe of an attorney-general to don the scarlet uniform as an aide-de-camp to the General. Brock addressed the Council, stating that he was convinced that at this juncture a bold and aggressive policy should be adopted. It was plain from the despatches and private correspondence taken from the enemy that the garrison of Detroit was in a state bordering on mutiny. General Hull appeared to have lost completely the confidence of his officers. Brock proposed, therefore, to cross the river, take up a strong position, and await the effect upon the enemy's camp, trusting that they would meet him in the field. If Hull refused to accept the challenge but remained behind his defences, the British commander proposed to storm the fort. He asked for the opinion of his officers on this plan of campaign.

Colonel Procter, who as Vice-President of the Council sat at the opposite end of the table, now arose and stated his views. In his opinion an attack upon Detroit would be a hopeless adventure. He pointed out to the General

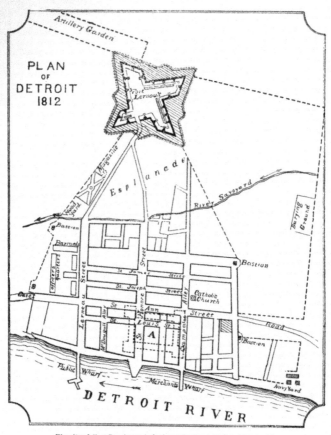

The site of Fort Ponchartrain is shown by the dotted enclosure, at A

PLAN OF DETROIT AND FORT LERNOULT, 1812

Brock and Tecumseh Meet

that the available British force consisted of, at the most, barely seven hundred men, only three hundred of these being regulars. The militia were an untried force, going into battle for the first time. They were poorly armed with the most nondescript weapons, but half clad and many of them even without shoes. It might be possible to muster six or seven hundred Indians, but these would be of little assistance in prosecuting a siege. They would soon tire of the monotony, and would spread over the country on expeditions of their own devising. The fort at Detroit was a very strong one, having been thoroughly overhauled during the year. The parapet was twenty feet in height, the thickness at the top being twelve feet. Surrounding the fort was a ditch six feet deep and at the bottom twelve feet wide. The palisades were made of new cedar pickets twelve inches in diameter. The fort was well supplied with artillery, having at least three dozen guns of various calibre, and the magazines were filled with ammunition of every kind. The garrison at present consisted of twenty-five hundred men, and the captured despatches showed that re-inforcements were expected from Ohio. In these circumstances, he submitted that it would be folly to make an attack on an enemy so superior in numbers and resources and occupying such a strong position.

One officer after another stated his views, the majority agreeing with Colonel Procter that an attempt against Fort Detroit would be hopeless. Quartermaster-General Nichol, with the Irishman's love for fighting, warmly supported the plans of the General. When all had spoken Brock rose, not to resume the debate but to announce his final decision: 123

The Story of Tecumseh

"Gentlemen," said the commander, "I have carefully weighed the pros and cons, and have fully made up my mind. We gain nothing by delay. We are committed to a war in which the enemy must always surpass us in numbers, equipment and resources. If the issue is to be determined by the rules of war we are already lost, but the history of our country furnishes many examples where the few being bold and courageous have overcome the many. I have definitely decided to cross the river. Instead of further advice from you I must beg of you to give me your hearty support. The general orders will be issued at once."

Turning to Tecumseh, who had listened with intense but closely veiled interest to the debate, Brock asked the chief for information as to the nature of the country surrounding Detroit. Taking a roll of elm bark, Tecumseh traced on the white inner surface with the point of his scalping-knife a map showing the hills, forests, rivers, roads, and trails with an exactness and amplitude of detail which would have done credit to an officer of the Royal Engineers.

Before dismissing the council, Brock invited Tecumseh to a great council to be held that day at noon. "That," said the General, looking at his watch, "will give us time for a few hours' sleep, as it is now after four o'clock."

Brock Demands the Surrender of Detroit

CHAPTER XVIII.

BROCK DEMANDS THE SURRENDER OF DETROIT.

By the following noon over one thousand Indians had assembled in a glade in the forest behind the fort—Ottawas, Chippewas, Wyandottes and Pottawatomies from Michigan and Ontario, Miamis and Shawanoes from Ohio and Indiana, Sacs and Foxes from the Iowa River country, Kickapoos from the prairies between the Illinois and the Mississippi, and Winnebagoes and Dacotahs from the far North-West, the fierce Horse Indians of the Plains. As the time fixed for the council drew near, the Indians seated themselves upon the ground, forming a half-circle, the members of each tribe grouped together. Under a great oak sat General Brock, the centre of a group of officers in brilliant uniforms. Between the Indians and the group of officers sat the chiefs. After the ceremonial pipe had passed, Brock rose to address the council. He told the grave red men that he had come to drive back the Longknives who had invaded the King's country. The Longknives were the enemies of the Indians and of the English; both, therefore, should join to fight them. The Americans had retreated to their own side of the river, but he intended to follow them, and if they would not come out and fight he would take their fort. The Americans had taken much land from the Indians, and were now trying to take the lands of the English also. If the English and the Indians

125

The Story of Tecumseh

made common cause against the Americans, they would soon drive them back beyond the old boundaries. When Brock had finished his address and resumed his seat, all eyes turned towards Tecumseh, who, after the customary pause, rose and spoke:

"Father, we have come here with the intention of informing you that we have not forgotten (we never can forget) what passed between you Englishmen and our ancestors. Your Fathers have nourished us and raised us up since childhood. We are now men. It would be a shame to us not to defend our country and yours. Father, the Longknives have done us great injury. We were about five years settled near Greenville, but they always suspected us of plotting mischief, so that we moved thence and settled on the Wabash. They suddenly came against us with a great force while I was absent, and destroyed our village and slew our warriors. We have fought the enemies of our Great Father the King, beyond the Great Lakes; they have never seen my back. We have come here to fight and take lessons from the English, so that we may learn to make war in these great forests. Father, we have a belt to show you which was given to our Kings when you laid the French on their back. Here it is, Father. On one end is your hand, on the other that of the red people, both hands in black wampum, but the Indian end of the white belt darker than the other, and in the middle the hearts of both. This belt, Father, our great chiefs have been sitting on ever since, keeping it concealed and ruining our country. Now the warriors have taken all the chiefs and turned their faces towards you, never again to look towards the Americans. Father, it is only recently I dis-

Brock Demands the Surrender of Detroit

covered this belt and took it from under our Kings. Father, I desire that this belt should be passed round and seen and handled by every Indian present. We will never quit our Father or let go his hand."

When Tecumseh resumed his seat, Roundhead, a tall and stately figure, splendid in barbaric adornment, rose to address the council. With the dignity that became his rank as head Chief of the Wyandottes, the Elder Brothers of all the Indian tribes, he said that Tecumseh, Chief of the Shawanoes, had spoken for all the red people. When the great Chief of the English had taken the hand of Tecumseh he had shaken the hands of a thousand Indians. When the council was over, presents were distributed amongst the Indians, including a supply of ammunition taken from the scanty store at the fort.

Next morning the little army marched up the river road to Sandwich, advance parties having been sent forward on the preceding day to prepare for their reception. Captain Dixon of the Royal Engineers had constructed batteries about three miles above Sandwich, directly opposite Detroit. These batteries were equipped with one 18-pounder, two 12½ and two 5½-inch mortars, and were screened by trees and underbrush so as to be completely hidden from the enemy, who had not been made aware of their existence. On the march the little army passed over the battered bridge at the Canard where the first shots of the war had been fired. The little river winding through the marshes seemed then, as it does to-day, far removed from scenes of strife and bloodshed. As they rode along Brock asked Tecumseh to see that firewater was kept from his people, and to prevent any barbarities on the

127

The Story of Tecumseh

part of the Indians. Tecumseh made answer that the Indians had promised not to touch pernicious spirits until the Longknives were humbled, and that he would not permit and never had permitted any atrocity to be committed.

Arrived at Sandwich, Brock took up his quarters in the old Bàby mansion. Sandwich, before the coming of the white men, had been the site of a Huron or Wyandotte village. Hither had come, in 1723, Fathers Richardie and Poitiers to establish a mission amongst the Hurons. They were Jesuits, members of that devoted company whose apostolic labours in behalf of the red men are, more than any feat of arms, the glory of the French race in Canada. They had found a country clothed in " groves of walnuts, chestnuts and stately oaks, trunks straight as arrows without knots, and almost without branches save at their very tops, growing with the lustiness of centuries upon them. Clouds of turkeys rose from the water's edge, wild swans swam in the lagoons and herds of deer roamed the forest." The scene had changed when Brock marched into Sandwich. The forest had given way to comfortable homes, prosperous farms, orchards and vineyards. A little town had grow around the mission of " L'Assomption," but in the grounds surrounding Colonel Bàby's house stood, as they stand to-day, the old French pear trees planted by the Jesuit missionaries.

> " Many a thrifty Mission pear
> Yet o'erlooks the blue St. Clair
> Like a veteran, faithful warden;
> And their branches, gnarled and olden,
> Still each year their blossoms dance,
> Scent and bloom of Sunny France."

Brock Demands the Surrender of Detroit

From headquarters at the Bàby mansion, Brock sent Colonel Macdonell and Captain Glegg under a flag of truce with a letter to General Hull, demanding the immediate surrender of Detroit. Meanwhile, the trees veiling Dixon's battery were felled and the underbrush cleared, preparatory to opening fire on the American fort. After some delay Macdonell and Glegg returned, bearing a letter from Hull in which he said that he was prepared to meet any forces which Brock had at his disposal. Brock immediately ordered the batteries to open fire on Detroit. For two hours this artillery duel lasted with little effect, and as evening fell the fire slackened and ceased. That night six hundred Indians under the leadership of Tecumseh launched their canoes on the dark waters and crossed to the American shore. Unperceived by the enemy, they spread out, completely surrounding the town and holding all the lines of communication. The American sentinels as they paced their rounds on the ramparts little dreamed that Detroit was already invested, surrounded by a cordon of enemies eager to avenge the wrongs they had suffered at the hands of the Longknives. The hoot of the owl and the plaintive cry of the whip-poor-will, the familiar night sounds of the forest, were the signals passed between the Indian scouts. In the council chamber of Fort Detroit the hours which should have been devoted to planning the defence of the post were wasted in fierce recriminations among the officers. Confidence in the commandant had been lost, and something approaching anarchy reigned. Meanwhile, a mile away across the river, lay another camp, and a force which bivouacked upon its arms.

The Story of Tecumseh

CHAPTER XIX.

GENERAL HULL SURRENDERS.

IN the early dawn of Sunday, August 16th, 1812, the inspiring call of the bugles roused the British camp. The moment for action had arrived. Dixon's battery three miles up the river began to speak, and the first shells, bursting directly over Fort Detroit, showed that the gunners had now obtained the range. The fort replied, but without effect. The British force, consisting of three hundred and thirty regulars and four hundred militia, assembled in the yard of the old stone school-house opposite St. John's Church. Three hundred of the militia were clothed in cast-off uniforms of the 41st Regiment, thus doubling in the enemy's eyes the number of regulars. Marching down to the water's edge, the troops embarked in boats and scows which had been provided as transports. The hardy river men of Sandwich had volunteered their services in rowing the boats across the mile-wide stretch of the Detroit River between the Canadian and American shores. The boats pushed out into the stream, followed by cheers and by the silent, though no less fervent, prayers of the women and old men assembled at the water's edge. Major Richardson, who was present, thus described the scene on that summer morning long ago:

" A soft August sun was just rising as we gained the

General Hull Surrenders

centre of the river, and the view at the moment was certainly very animated and exciting, for amid the little squadron of boats and scows conveying the troops and artillery were mixed numerous canoes filled with warriors decorated in their half nakedness for the occasion, and uttering yells of mingled defiance of their foes and encouragement of the soldiery. Above us again were to be seen and heard the flashes and thunder of the artillery from our batteries, which, as on the preceding day, were but feebly replied to by the enemy, while the gay flags of the *Queen Charlotte,* drooping in the breezeless yet not oppressive air and playing on the calm surface of the river, seemed to give an earnest of success and inspired every bosom."

In the foremost boat stood General Brock erect, scanning with the aid of his field-glasses the opposite shore, alert for any indications of the enemy. The river at this point flows with great swiftness, and the powerful current rendered it impossible for the little flotilla to cross in a direct line, so that the landing was made at Springwells, about four miles below Detroit. Here, the bank of the river, which was about six feet high, had been scored and cut by the springs from which the place derived its name. This was a favourite camping-ground of the Indians. At a little distance from the river rose a number of irregularly shaped mounds, the ancient burial-ground of the Indian tribes. Tecumseh, sitting on his white mustang, surrounded by his Indians, awaited Brock's landing. As the Shawanoe chief greeted the General, one of the lesser chiefs stepped forward and, attracting Tecumseh's atten-

The Story of Tecumseh

tion, pointed south along the river road, speaking rapidly in the Shawanoe tongue. Tecumseh turned and looked in the direction indicated, shading his eyes with his hand. The keen-eyed chief perceived that what had appeared at first as but an eddy of dust stirred by the wind was a horseman riding at break-neck speed towards them. As the rider drew nearer he was recognized as one of Tecumseh's scouts. When the messenger reached the spot where Tecumseh stood, he reined in his horse sharply, and, leaping to the ground, presented himself before the chief. At a sign from the chief he spoke rapidly for some minutes, the British officers gathering closer, interested spectators of the episode, though the strange syllables fell without meaning upon their ears. When the messenger had withdrawn, Tecumseh, turning to Brock, said: "I reported to you yesterday that Colonel McArthur with five hundred cavalry had left Detroit to join Brush at the Raisin. This man of mine now tells me that McArthur is encamped on this road but three miles below us. We have need to make our plans quickly."

"This being the case," said Brock, "I shall attack Detroit at once. The force will move forward in three brigades, the men at double distance apart. The guns will follow immediately in rear of the First Brigade. Let officers make these dispositions without further delay."

Soon the little army was under way marching towards Detroit. At the head of his troops rode Major-General Brock on his grey charger, Tecumseh by his side. On one side of the road flowed the broad river, its surface sparkling in the morning sunlight. On the other side

132

General Hull Surrenders

were neat, whitewashed farm-houses standing close together in neighborly propinquity, according to the custom
of the French-Canadian farmers. Ahead, on the left of the
road, ran the Indians, circling about through orchard,
field and vineyard for the purpose of uncovering any un-
seen foe. Three bridges were crossed, and Knagg's stone
windmill, its sails motionless in the quiet air, was passed.
Beyond, the road climbed upward to the entrance to the
town. From this ridge the muzzles of six heavy guns
pointed down the Springwells road. Steadily the little
force marched on to the measured roll of the drums.
Nearer and nearer they approached the American battery.
The gunners could now be perceived with lighted fuses
in their hands awaiting the command to fire. It seemed,
indeed, that the gallant little band were marching into
"the jaws of death," but no man faltered, though every eye
was fixed upon the frowning guns. One man, indeed, felt
fear, but not for himself. Colonel Nichol, pressing forward, saluted Brock and said:

"Pardon me, General, but I cannot forbear entreating
you not to expose yourself thus. If we lose you we lose all,
but we pray you to allow the troops to pass on, led by their
own officers."

The reply he received was: "I will never ask my troops
to go where I do not lead them." This characteristic
answer recalls Tecumseh's criticism of Brock and Procter:
"General Brock says 'Come,' General Procter says 'Go.'"

Still the American batteries remained strangely silent.
The tension grew almost too great to be borne, as the
little army still pressed steadily forward, marching appar-

133

The Story of Tecumseh

ently straight into a cul-de-sac. When within about one-quarter mile of the fort, a sharp order ran down the line, and deploying to the left, the little army marched through an orchard and halted about three hundred yards from the road, near a farm-house. In this position the troops were covered.

Meanwhile, things had been going badly in Fort Detroit. While the passage of the river was being effected by Brock, Dixon's battery had been steadily pounding the fort. One shell entering through an embrasure killed four officers, one of whom was Lieutenant Hanks, who had commanded at Mackinaw at the time of the surrender of Captain Roberts. Hull became completely demoralized by this disaster and resolved to surrender. Without consulting his officers, he despatched a flag of truce to Sandwich with proposals for a conference which should arrange terms of capitulation.

Brock was already marching along the Springwells road towards Detroit when Hull's emissary returned with Captain Dixon's message referring Hull to General Brock for an answer. On General Brock's approach Hull withdrew his forces into the fort, with the exception of the detachment which occupied the battery on the Springwells road. To the officer in command of the battery Hull gave strict injunctions not to fire on the British. This explained the silence of the guns. Leaving his troops in the orchard, General Brock, with Tecumseh and his aides-de-camp, Colonel Macdonell and Major Glegg, rode to the brow of the rising ground for the purpose of reconnoitering the fort. As they looked, a gate opened and an officer bearing a

General Hull Surrenders

white flag issued forth. Brock immediately despatched his aides to meet the flag. Colonel Glegg returned at full gallop, and, reining his horse back upon his haunches, saluted: "A flag, sir, from General Hull, proposing negotiations for the surrender of Detroit." Not a muscle of Brock's face moved as he looked into the eyes of his aide, but who can say what thoughts raced through his brain as he saw the fruition of his great dream. "I depute you and Colonel Macdonell to arrange the terms of capitulation." With a parting salute Major Glegg wheeled his horse about and galloped to the spot where Colonel Macdonell and the American officer awaited him. The heavy gate of the fort swung open and the three officers entered.

Across the river in Sandwich, at the hour of morning service, the bell of old St. Johns rang out its accustomed summons to prayer. The white-haired rector, the Reverend Richard Pollard, looked down over his congregation. Fathers, mothers and sisters were there, but the sons were with the forlorn hope before Detroit. Through the open windows the soft summer breeze, laden with the scent of flower and field, stole into the little church. All was peace and quiet. Muffled and indistinct from the river came the sound of guns, portents of evil import, which fell heavily on the heart. With trembling voice the aged rector read the prayer, "In time of war and tumult, save and deliver us, we humbly beseech thee, from the hands of our enemies, abate their pride, assuage their malice, and confound their devices, that we being armed with thy defence may be preserved evermore from all perils to glorify thee, who art the only Giver of victory."

The Story of Tecumseh

Meanwhile, at Detroit the terms of capitulation were being arranged, and at noon were signed by the respective commanders. The territory of Michigan, Fort Detroit, thirty-seven pieces of ordnance, one hundred thousand cartridges, two thousand five hundred stand-of-arms and the armed brig *Adams* were ceded to the British. Two thousand five hundred American soldiers became prisoners of war. The British marched through the orchards and fields to the fort, where they formed on the glacis. Above them from the embrasures in the thick walls frowned the heavy guns, silent in the presence of the conquerors. British sentinels were placed at the gates and about the ramparts. The American troops, now prisoners of war, sullenly issued from the fort and formed on the esplanade. They felt the natural resentment of brave men at the cowardice of their commander.

Brock and Tecumseh entered the fort, followed by the soldiers, the Indians remaining outside. Brock, turning to Tecumseh, asked him to protect the Americans from the Indians. "We Indians," said Tecumseh, "despise the Longknives too much to touch them." The Stars and Stripes descended from the peak of the flagstaff of the fort, and the Union Jack was run up amid the thundering salutes of the captured guns. From the river the *Queen Charlotte*, as she sailed past the fort with flags and streamers floating proudly in the breeze, re-echoed the salute. Cheer after cheer went up from the soldiers. In the fort were several brass guns bearing the inscription, " Surrendered by Cornwallis at Saratoga." In the excitement of the moment the British officers with tears in their eyes

General Hull Surrenders

kissed the recaptured guns. Outside the fort the Indians, shouting and leaping, discharged their firearms in the air, giving way to the most extravagant manifestations of joy. From the tower of old St. Ann's the bells rang out a peal of victory. Tecumseh, when the excitement had somewhat subsided, turned to Brock and said: " I have heard much of your fame, and am happy to shake again by the hand a brave brother warrior. We have been the witnesses of your valour. In crossing the river to attack the enemy, we observed you from a distance standing erect the whole time, and when the boat reached the shore you were among the first who jumped on land. Your bold and sudden movement alarmed the enemy, and compelled them to surrender to less than half their own force." Brock, in turn, shaking the chief's hand, expressed again the great indebtedness of the British to their Indian allies. Untying his silken sash, he threw it over Tecumseh's shoulders, and at the same time presented him with a brace of silver-mounted pistols handsomely chased. The gallant chief, not to be outdone in courtesy, gave Brock his own Red River sash. This the General wore until the day of his death, a few months later, on the heights of Queenston. However, much as Tecumseh valued the silken sash as an evidence of Brock's regard, he did not retain it long in his possession. The next day Brock noticed that the chief was not wearing it, and thinking that perhaps he had unwittingly offended his ally, asked why it had been discarded. Tecumseh replied that he had presented the sash to Roundhead, a much abler chief than himself. By this simple act of diplomacy he completely won the heart

The Story of Tecumseh

of Roundhead, who, as Sarstantzee of the Wyandotte Confederation, exercised a great influence over the Indians.

In his report to the Secretary of War, written after the fall of Detroit, Hull justified the surrender of the Fort by stating that the Indians had cut off his supplies from Ohio and ambushed the expeditions sent out to re-establish communications. He grossly exaggerated the number of Indians, of whom he stood in the greatest terror, stating that a vast number of red men of almost every tribe and nation in the West and North-West had joined the British.

There can be little question that Brock would have been unsuccessful in his bold attempt on Detroit had it not been for the presence and active co-operation of Tecumseh and his braves. Major Glegg started immediately for Quebec, bearing General Brock's despatches to the Commander-in-Chief, and taking with him as trophies of victory the Fort Standard and the colours of the 4th United States Regiment, the "Heroes of Tippecanoe." These colours were afterwards deposited in the Chapel Royal, Whitehall, thence they were removed to the Royal Hospital, Chelsea, where they now hang amid other "relics of an age of war."

Lieutenant George Ryerson, of the First Norfolk Militia, a mere boy, set out with despatches to the Talbot settlement near St. Thomas. All day long he rode through the thick woods along the River Thames. When night fell he still pressed on, unconscious of fatigue. Darker and darker grew the woods and more difficult the way. At last he perceived through the trees the glimmer of a fire. Dismounting from his weary horse, he took the bridle in his hand, and stumbling on through the night at last found

BABY MANSION, SANDWICH

Built 1799   Headquarters for Generals Brock, Hull, Proctor, Tecumseh, Harrison

General Hull Surrenders

himself on the edge of an open glade in the forest looking down on an Indian encampment. There were many wigwams, but around the fire which blazed high in the midst were gathered only a few women, children and aged men. All the warriors were with Tecumseh at Detroit. Ryerson was welcomed with the hospitality for which the Indian is distinguished. The good news was quickly told. All night long the old warriors, seated about the fire, their wrinkled faces shining with war-paint, chanted their songs of victory.

The Story of Tecumseh

CHAPTER XX.

THE SUCCESS AT FRENCHTOWN.

The news of the fall of Detroit was received throughout the whole extent of Canada with almost incredulous joy. It seemed to the Canadians hardly possible that a victory so important and so far-reaching in effect could be achieved by the little army of the West against an enemy so vastly superior in numbers and resources. Not only had the invader been driven from Canada, but a large expanse of territory had been ceded to the British. Over the strongest forts of the Americans in the North and West, Mackinaw and Detroit, floated the Union Jack. Fresh courage inspired every bosom, doubters were convinced and traitors silenced. Brock was hailed by all as the saviour and defender of Upper Canada. The Americans were almost stupefied by this blow to their national pride. They were learning the lesson "that a country defended by free men, enthusiastically devoted to the cause of their King and constitution, could never be conquered." On the 18th of August, General Brock set sail in the schooner *Chippewa* for Fort George. He had determined to make an aggressive campaign on the Niagara frontier. At Sackett's Harbour on Lake Ontario, the enemy were fitting out a fleet with which they hoped to defeat Sir James Yeo and thus obtain the command of the lake. Brock was

The Success at Frenchtown

well informed concerning the plans of the Americans, and intended to lead an expedition against Sackett's Harbour and destroy the shipyards and the vessels of the enemy. Unfortunately for Canada, the imbecility of Prevost blocked this well-laid plan.

During Brock's short stay at Detroit he had seen much of Tecumseh, whom he greatly admired. In a letter to Lord Liverpool he said: " He who attracted most of my attention was a Shawanoe chief, Tecumseh, brother to the Prophet. A more sagacious or more gallant warrior does not exist. He was the admiration of every one who conversed with him." Tecumseh little thought, as he watched the white sails of the *Chippewa* fading from sight, that he had seen the last of his friend. Less than two months later, the gallant Brock fell at Queenston Heights while repulsing an invasion of the enemy.

Things being for the moment at a standstill on the western Canadian border, Tecumseh set out for the Wabash to recruit reinforcements amongst the tribes of that region.

General Harrison, who was in command of the American forces in the West, with headquarters at Urbana, Ohio, despatched General Winchester with a force of two thousand five hundred men against the Indians. After destroying the villages on the Miami, burning the food supplies of the Indians and driving the women and children into the forest, Winchester established himself on the Miami, where he built a fort called, after the Governor of Ohio, Fort Meigs. Procter, anxious to watch Winchester's movements, established an outpost at Frenchtown

141

The Story of Tecumseh

(now Monroe), on the Raisin, about eighteen miles distant from Amherstburg. Major Reynolds of the Essex militia, who was placed in command, had a force of fifty white men and two hundred Indians. He had also one three-pounder.

In January, 1813, Winchester sent Colonel Lewis with a force of eight hundred men to surprise the little garrison at Frenchtown. Reynolds' Indian scouts had brought him intelligence of the approach of the enemy, so that he was not taken unawares. The militia behaved with great gallantry, repeatedly forcing the enemy to take shelter in the woods, but the odds were too great. Reynolds was forced to retire, which he did in good order, carrying off his little gun. Lewis, who had been roughly handled by the Canadians, showed no disposition to pursue.

Procter, on receiving Reynolds' report, acted with decision and energy. He surmised that Winchester would bring up his main force and proceed to fortify Frenchtown. He resolved to attack at once, and on the 19th of January, leaving only a corporal's guard at Amherstburg, set out for Frenchtown. Procter's force consisted of five hundred regulars and militia and about eight hundred Indians, the latter being led in Tecumseh's absence by the Wyandotte chief, Roundhead. Lieutenant Richardson, who was with the expedition, has left us the following interesting description of the starting of the little army on its hazardous adventure:

"No sight could be more beautiful than the departure of this little army from Amherstburg. It was the depth of winter. The river at the point where we crossed was four

The Success at Frenchtown

miles in breadth. The deep rumbling noise of the guns, prolonging their reverberations like the roar of distant thunder as they moved along the ice, mingled with the wild cries of the Indians, seemed to threaten some convulsion of nature, while the appearance of the troops winding along the road, now lost behind some cliff, or rugged ice, now emerging into view, their polished arms glittering in the sunbeams, gave an air of romantic grandeur to the scene. On the night of the 21st, the invading force made camp within five miles of Frenchtown. The cold was so intense that great fires were kindled. Around these fires couches were made of branches of fir and balsam. With no covering save their great-coats, the wearied soldiers laid down to rest. In the clear winter sky the stars shone with unusual brilliance; all was still save for the crunch of snow under the foot of the sentry as he paced his rounds, and the crackling of the forest trees in the frost. Two hours before dawn the camp was roused. Around the blazing fires the soldiers gathered to partake of the morning meal, after which the little army formed along the road. The order, 'Quick march,' was given, and the expedition was once more under way, winding through the forest on the Frenchtown trail. An hour later Frenchtown was reached.

" The American camp was dark and silent. No sentry challenged as the invading force emerged ghost-like from the dark rim of the forest. The surprise was complete. The Americans were lying in their beds, undressed and unarmed. A prompt advance of the British line would have decided the issue at once. Instead, Procter ordered the artillery to open fire on the American camp, thus giving the defenders time to arm and form behind the breastworks. By this extraordinary manoeuvre he abandoned all the advantage he had obtained in surprising the enemy. All now depended on the courage and tenacity of the attacking troops. Winchester with the main body of his army had left Fort Meigs, and joined Lewis at Frenchtown on the 20th, the day after Procter set out from Amherstburg. The American force was therefore much superior to the British. Resting their rifles on the parapet, the Americans directed a brisk fire against the British centre, thus holding them in check. The light was growing stronger. The British in their regular formation stood out in dark lines against the snow-covered ground, forming an excellent mark for the American riflemen. On the right, the militia and Indians were more successful, driving back the enemy, who fled in confusion. The Indians pursued the fugitives for over two miles, inflicting great loss. Winchester, who led this division in person, was taken prisoner by Roundhead and brought to Procter, who had in the meantime occupied the ground abandoned by the American right, thus outflanking the American position. On the successful completion of this manoeuvre, the breastworks were abandoned by the enemy, who now threw themselves into a blockhouse and there continued a desperate resistance. Winchester, however, having learned the state of the action, wrote an order to the officer commanding the blockhouse instructing him to surrender his troops as prisoners of war. Colonel Procter despatched an officer under a flag of truce to deliver this

THE OLD MORAVIAN MISSION CHURCH

Delaware Indian Reserve

The Success at Frenchtown

order. The defenders thereupon issued from the block-house and surrendered."

The battle of Frenchtown was fought and won. The British loss was twenty-four killed and one hundred and fifty-eight wounded; that of the enemy, three hundred killed and five hundred and seventy-two wounded and taken prisoners. The remainder of the Americans effected their escape to Fort Miami.

The Story of Tecumseh

CHAPTER XXI.

BATTLES ON THE MAUMEE.

TECUMSEH'S mission to the Indians along the Wabash was crowned with success. He held councils in the various villages through which he passed, and soon gathered a large number of eager volunteers. The news of the capture of Detroit had already reached these tribes, and the announcement by Tecumseh of the British success at Frenchtown, which had been reported to him by a runner despatched by Roundhead, convinced the Indians that the issue of the war was no longer uncertain. Great Britain was their natural ally, and enlistment in her service would ensure to them a share in the spoils belonging to the victors. Tecumseh received so many offers of assistance that he became apprehensive that the commissariat at Amherstburg would be unable to provide food for the Indians who were journeying thither. He directed, therefore, that the warriors should be divided into two bands, one of which was to proceed to Amherstburg at once. The other band was to remain on the Wabash, holding itself in readiness to attack Harrison's rear should he make any movement against Detroit.

Having made these arrangements, Tecumseh felt that he was free to rejoin his immediate followers at Amherstburg. The homeward trail led by the Maumee, and

Battles on the Maumee

Tecumseh determined to ascertain if possible the nature of Harrison's plans. Arriving in the vicinity of Fort Meigs, he learned that Harrison had determined to winter there, preparatory to an early spring campaign against Detroit, reinforcements having been promised him from Kentucky. He found that Harrison had transformed the rough outpost into a regular fortification. The walls had been enlarged and strengthened, and blockhouses were in course of construction. Tecumseh hastened to Amherstburg, where he informed Procter of the conditions on the Maumee, and urged him to move against Fort Meigs at once, before the fortifications were completed and the expected reinforcements arrived.

It was not, however, until the 23rd of April that Procter could be prevailed upon to set out. The British expedition consisted of nine hundred and eighty-three white troops, half of whom were militia, and twelve hundred Indians under Tecumseh. The Indians journeyed overland, while the soldiers were transported by water. Procter had with him two small gunboats, the *Eliza* and the *Meyers*. They were of light draught, and could ascend the Maumee and assist in the siege. The artillery, with the exception of two 24-pounders captured at Detroit, was too light to be effective.

On the 1st of May the British landed and opened up a battery on the left bank of the river opposite the fort. This battery bombarded the fort for four days without intermission. The British artillery was well served, and almost completely silenced the American guns. The fire of the 24-pounders was concentrated upon the traverse

The Story of Tecumseh

and magazine, but with little effect. The flank companies of the 41st Regiment, supported by a few Indians, constructed a small battery close to the north end of the fort. Meanwhile, General Clay with one thousand five hundred Kentuckians was descending the Maumee to join Harrison. Just before Procter's arrival Harrison had received word of Clay's proximity. After the investment of the fort by the British, Harrison sent a courier who managed to evade the Indian scouts and reached Clay. In his letter to Clay, Harrison advised him of the condition of affairs at Fort Meigs, and ordered him to land on the left bank, surprise the main batteries, spike the guns and then retire immediately to the fort. Harrison promised to make a sortie from the fort against the smaller battery.

Early in the morning of the 5th of May, the American flotilla, consisting of eighteen flatboats with shields on the sides as protection from the bullets of the Indians, arrived in the vicinity of the fort. Under cover of the morning's mists which hung over the river, eight hundred and sixty-six men under Colonel Dudley were landed on the British side of the river, a short distance above the batteries. The landing was not perceived by the British. Circling around, the Americans attacked from the rear and carried the position, the few artillerymen, who were unsupported, being incapable of making an effective resistance. Having so easily accomplished his object, and elated by his success, Dudley, after spiking the guns, continued to hold the ground vacated by the British.

The British camp was situated about one mile further down the river, near the ruins of old Fort Miami. Thither

Battles on the Maumee

ran the fugitives from the captured battery, and gave the alarm. Tecumseh had seen from the opposite side of the river the American attack on the battery. Without hesitating an instant, he and his Indians swam the river and advanced against the enemy. Dudley with the main body of the Americans moved forward to meet Tecumseh, leaving Major Shelby with about one hundred men in charge of the battery.

The weather had been cold and wet. The rain now began to fall in torrents. Down the road on the double, knee-deep in mud, came the men of the 41st, eager to retake the battery. Major Chambers, Lieutenants Bullock, Clements and Richardson, with twelve men of the rank and file, outstripped their companions in the race. When they came in sight of the battery, over which the Stars and Stripes was waving, Major Chambers called in stentorian tones, "Who'll follow me and retake that battery?" With a cheer the gallant little band, without waiting for their comrades, charged the position with fixed bayonets. The Americans, after delivering one volley, turned and fled. When the remainder of the 41st under Major Muir came up, they found their men in possession of the battery, and turned their attention to the conflict being waged between Tecumseh and Dudley. Attacked in the rear, the Americans were driven backward and forward between the forces of Muir and Tecumseh. After suffering severely the Americans surrendered, only about one hundred and fifty making good their escape. The prisoners taken numbered five hundred men.

General Clay with the remainder of his forces had

The Story of Tecumseh

landed on the left bank of the river. Here he was attacked by the Indians, and fought his way through to the fort, losing a number of his boats. When Harrison saw that the main battery had been captured by Dudley, he ordered Colonel Miller to make a sortie against the smaller battery near the fort. Miller with a force of three hundred and fifty men issued from the fort, and captured the battery, which was held by a company of the 41st and a few militia, numbering in all one hundred and thirty men. Hardly, however, had Miller effected his object when a body of Canadian militia charged the Americans, recaptured the guns and drove Miller back to the fort, with a loss of twenty-eight killed and twenty-five wounded. The total loss of the Americans on both sides of the river, including prisoners, amounted to eight hundred and thirty-six men. Procter's loss was twenty killed and forty-one wounded.

At the height of the action some prisoners from the fort under Dudley were marched down the river road, the intention being to place them on the gunboats for safe-keeping. When some distance from the battle-ground the guard was forced by a band of dissolute Indians who had taken no part in the engagement. These wretches proceeded to massacre the unfortunate prisoners. Sergeant Russell, of the 41st, was shot through the heart while engaged in defending the Americans. Word was sent to Tecumseh, who immediately rode up at full gallop, followed by a few of his retinue. Raising his tomahawk above his head, he shouted, " Begone, dogs, or I will destroy you! " Tecumseh's presence was of instant effect; the baffled savages slunk away into the forest.

OLD FORT, AMHERSTBURG

Battles on the Maumee

The British victory, was, however, a barren one. Over Fort Meigs still waved the Stars and Stripes. The fire of the besiegers seemed to have little effect upon the defences; the shells, sinking into the wet clay of the traverse, failed to explode. The weather continued wet and cold. Since the men lacked even the shelter of tents, dysentery and fever ran riot in the British camp. The Indians, enriched by the plunder taken from the captured boats, wished, as was their custom, to return home with their spoils and their wounded. Day after day their numbers diminished. Tecumseh, chafing at the inaction, sent a letter to Harrison: "Come out and give me battle. You talked like a brave when I met you at Vincennes, and I respected you, but now you hide behind logs and in the earth like a groundhog. Give me answer." Procter, however, now decided to raise the siege. He retired in good order with all his cannon and stores of every description, arriving at Amherstburg without further adventure.

It was well known that the Americans were fitting out a powerful fleet at Erie, but the English commander made no attempt to frustrate their plans, though he must have known that it was of vital importance that the British supremacy on the lakes should be maintained. Amherstburg was doomed the moment the enemy obtained command on the waters of Lake Erie. Tecumseh, however, urged Procter to make a second attempt against Fort Meigs. He suggested that as the place had proved too strong to be carried by assault, it might be taken by strategy. He had learned that General Clay was in command, Harrison having gone into camp at Lower San-

The Story of Tecumseh

dusky, about thirty miles by the river road from Fort Meiggs. His plan was an ingenious one. He proposed that the Indian force under his command and a company of militia should be landed some distance below the fort. The Indians and militia were to take up a position on the Sandusky road, unperceived by the defenders of the fort. The British troops were to lie in ambush close to the walls. When these preparations had been completed, the militia and the Indians were to engage in a sham battle, which would lead the Americans within the fort to think that reinforcements had been attacked by the Indians. The troops would, it was thought, make a sortie in favour of their friends. When the relief party had crossed the open ground, the British were to rise from ambush and rush the fort before the gates could be effectively closed.

Procter thought that the scheme gave a fair promise of success, and late in July set out from Amherstburg on this the second expedition against Fort Meigs. He had with him about three hundred troops and a few pieces of artillery. Tecumseh's Indians numbered about one thousand. The British troops were disembarked at some distance from the fort, and took up the position agreed on, apparently without alarming the enemy. Not long afterwards heavy firing was heard on the Sandusky road. So realistic was the sham battle that the British troops were half in doubt as to whether Tecumseh had not really come into contact with some of Harrison's forces. At the sound of firing, the ramparts of the fort were lined with soldiers, who looked anxiously towards the road and excitedly dis-

Battles on the Maumee

cussed the situation. No movement, however, was made to sally from the fort. It is probable that the experience of General Clay and his troops at the first siege made them very chary about venturing out.

Chagrined at the failure of this plan, Procter determined to make an attempt against Fort Stephenson on the Sandusky River. Fort Stephenson consisted of block-houses, connected by a double stockade, skirted by a deep ditch. Procter arrived before Fort Stephenson on the 1st of August, and opened his batteries the next day. In planning the expedition it had not been contemplated that any frontal attack should be made on a fort. Procter's artillery consisted of light field guns, and no ladders or fascines had been provided. Nevertheless, after firing all day on the north-west angle of the fort, Procter ordered an assault. The task which Procter had given his soldiers was an impossible one, but they responded without hesitation and advanced on the fort. A few axes had been brought, but these through long service were so blunt as to be of little use. Leaping into the ditch, the axemen hacked at the stout palings, but with little effect. The troops, unable to scale the walls, were swept down by a murderous fire without being able to retaliate on the enemy and without the slightest hope of accomplishing the object of the attack. For nearly two hours the unequal contest waged. Then " Cease fire " sounded, and the wearied troops, lying on the ground, waited for darkness. About nine o'clock the British forces withdrew, having lost twenty-six killed and thirty-nine wounded and not having

The Story of Tecumseh

secured for themselves the slightest advantage. Tecumseh with his Indians had been stationed on the Sandusky road, with the object of preventing Harrison bringing up troops to the assistance of the garrison, and thus took no part in the engagement. Procter with the remainder of his forces re-embarked, and on the 9th of August reached Amherstburg.

TECUMSEH STONE, AMHERSTBURG

Tecumseh Counsels Continued War

CHAPTER XXII.

TECUMSEH COUNSELS CONTINUED WAR.

THE British fleet of six ships under Captain Barclay, R.N., had held command of Lake Erie since the opening of the war. In August, 1813, Captain Perry set sail from Erie with a well equipped and powerful fleet of nine vessels, resolved to win for the Americans supremacy upon the lakes. Barclay's ships, then lying at Amherstburg, were badly rigged and poorly armed. His flagship, the *Detroit*, was launched in an unfurnished condition. No naval guns having been sent forward, the fort was practically stripped of guns to furnish her armament. There were only fifty able seamen in the British fleet. The remainder of the crews consisted of lake sailors and men of the 41st Regiment. Early in September the situation had grown critical. The garrison was on half rations. Starvation stared them in the face. Barclay resolved to go out and meet the enemy. It was, indeed, the only course open to him. On the 10th of September, 1813, the rival fleets engaged off the Sister Islands. After a fierce and sanguinary conflict the British fleet was overpowered, and all the ships captured. The crippled fleet, victors and vanquished, crept into Put-in Bay, where they lay at anchor during the night. Next morning the funeral service was read, and a procession of boats slowly made its

The Story of Tecumseh

way to the land, while the minute-guns sounded the requiem. The day was clear and bright, the lake calm, all nature was at peace, as the victims of war were laid to their last rest in the shade of the solemn woods which darkly fringed the shore.

Desperate, indeed, was now the position of Amherstburg and Detroit. Provisions were almost exhausted. Already Procter had been forced to kill many of his horses to provide food for his Indian allies, the troops were in rags and tatters, winter was coming on, the pay of the soldiers was long in arrears. The victorious fleet of the enemy held the lake, and might at any time appear before the fort, accompanied by the powerful force which Harrison had gathered at the Maumee. A courier, bearing despatches from Prevost, arrived at Amherstburg, having travelled overland. The despatches announced that sailors were on their way to reinforce the fleet, and that the long-promised armament for the *Detroit* had reached Burlington. This news, which but a few days before would have meant the salvation of the West, now but added to the bitterness of the hour. Had these reinforcements, so long promised, reached Amherstburg in time, there is little question but that a crowning British victory on Lake Erie would have resulted.

Prevost had once more shown his incapacity for the position he occupied. Yet he had the audacity, when later on he learned of Barclay's defeat, to censure the unfortunate Procter for advising Barclay to go out against the enemy before the arrival of these reinforcements. Procter had written Prevost months before, remonstrating with him in language as plain as a subordinate could use to the Commander-in-Chief: "Your Excellency will perceive that the reinforcements you intended I should have long since received have not been sent, nor do I expect to receive any whilst any circumstance may seem to justify their detention." Later on, after Perry's fleet had left Erie, he again entreated Prevost to send seamen, telling him plainly that anything regrettable which might happen would be due to his neglect in sending the aid which was so much needed. Procter had not told the Indians of Barclay's defeat, but Tecumseh surmised the truth, and was insistent that the commander should take him into his confidence. Having given the fullest proof of his devotion to the British cause, which was indeed his own, the chief had a right to be informed of the true position of affairs and to have a voice in the decision which must at once be arrived at.

It was not, however, until the 18th of September that Procter called a council at the council house of the Amherstburg Indian Agency. The walls and lofty vaulted roof, stained black with age, had looked down on many historic meetings between the representatives of the Great Father over the Seas and his red children. None rivalled in importance the meeting which was about to take place. As the appointed hour drew near, the Indians began to assemble before the council house. General Procter made his way through the throng, accompanied by Colonel Matthew Elliott. Colonel Warburton, Colonel Evans, Major Chambers, Major Muir, Captain Dixon of the Royal Engineers and other officers were present, all dressed as if

The Story of Tecumseh

for parade. General Procter took his seat in the great chair at the end of the room under the Royal Arms, while the officers grouped themselves about the walls, the brilliant scarlet of their uniforms standing out vividly against the dark background. The Indians entered the hall, their moccasined feet making no sound. Spreading their blankets, they seated themselves crosslegged upon the floor. Shawanoes, Saukies, Sioux, Miamis, Chippewas, Foxes, Ottawas and Pottawatomies, by tribes they took their places. The chiefs—Tecumseh, the Prophet, Naudee, Shaubena, Black Hawk, Roundhead and Split Log—sat at the head of their respective nations. The time-honoured formalities having been observed, Procter rose to state his plans. He spake thus: " Listen, my children. You know that our ships have gone out to meet the Longknives, but where they are now we do not know. You know, too, that we gave Barclay the great guns of the fort which shoot the double balls, and much powder and more provisions than we could well spare. We sent many of the soldiers from the fort with the fleet that they might fight the King's enemies, who are also your own. We have received word that Harrison is gathering a great army, in number as the leaves of the forest, and intends to set out from the Maumee and fight us here. We cannot fight without food, and when his great guns speak we have none to answer them. How then can we make a stand against this great army who lack nothing, and we so few and lacking all things ? Let us therefore burn the forts at Amherstburg and Detroit and all the buildings, and fall back overland towards Niagara, so that the enemy when they come

158

will find nothing. If they should follow us, we will lead them on into our own country far from their ships, where we will be joined by many of the King's soldiers. We can then turn and destroy them. This is my plan. Is it good in your ears, my children?"

There was silence for some moments after Procter resumed his seat. Then Tecumseh arose. Dressed in a close-fitting buckskin suit which revealed the athletic proportions of his frame, a large ostrich plume overshadowing his brow, the silver medal, his sole ornament, rising and falling upon his breast, indicative of the passion which inspired him, he made a figure at once imposing and wild. His piercing eyes swept for a moment the lines of his people, who leaned forward tense with excitement, eager to catch every word which fell from his lips. Then turning to Procter he began his speech. As he proceeded with his address he relaxed the restraint which he had placed upon his feelings, and his powerful voice rang through the council hall:

"Father, listen to your children. You see them now all before you. The war before this our British Father gave the hatchet to his red children when our old chiefs were alive. They are now all dead. In that war our Father was thrown on his back by the Americans, and our Father took them by the hand without our knowledge, and we are afraid that our Father will do so again at this time. Summer before last, when I came forward with my red brethren and was ready to take up the hatchet in favour of our Father, we were told not to be in a hurry, that he had not yet determined to fight the Americans.

The Story of Tecumseh

" Listen! You told us at that time to bring forward our families to this place. We did so, and you promised to take care of them, and that they should want for nothing while our men fought the enemy. You told us we were not to trouble ourselves with the garrisons of the enemy, that we knew nothing about them, and that our Father would attend to that part of the business. You also told your red children that you would take good care of the garrison here, which made our hearts glad.

" Listen! When we last went to the rapids of the Maumee, it is true we gave you little assistance. It is hard to fight people who live like groundhogs.

" Father, listen! Our fleet has gone out, we know they have fought, we have heard the great guns, but know nothing of what has happened to our Father with one arm (Barclay). Our ships have gone one way, and we are much astonished to see our Father tying up everything and preparing to run away the other, without letting his red children know what his intentions really are. You always told us to remain here and take care of our lands. It made our hearts glad to hear that such was your wish. Our Great Father the King is the head, and you represent him. You always told us you would never draw your foot off British ground, but now, Father, we see that you are giving way, and that without seeing the enemy. We must compare our Father's conduct to a fat animal that carried its tail upon its back, but when affrighted drops it between its legs and runs off.

" Listen, Father! The Americans have not yet defeated us by land, neither are we sure that they have done so by

Tecumseh Counsels Continued War

water. We therefore wish to remain here and fight our enemies. If they defeat us we will then retreat with our Father. At the battle of the Rapids (Fallen Timbers) last war, the Americans certainly defeated us, and when we retreated to our Father's fort the gates were shut against us. We were afraid that it would now be the case, but instead we see our Father preparing to march out of his garrison.

"Father!" he thundered, "you have the arms and the ammunition which our Great Father sent for his red children. If you intend going away, give them to us and you may go. Our lives are in the hands of the Great Spirit. We are determined to defend our lands, and if it be his will we wish to leave our bones upon them."

Hardly had the last words of Tecumseh reverberated through the chamber when the Indians sprang to their feet, brandishing their tomahawks and shouting in a dozen languages their approval of Tecumseh's plan. If Procter's heart fluttered in his bosom, he concealed his trepidation, and sat apparently unmoved throughout the tumult. When at last silence was restored, Procter addressed himself to Tecumseh, for the first time giving a frank and detailed account of his position, the defeat of Barclay and the urgent necessity of abandoning Amherstburg. Tecumseh finally consented to follow Procter, but stipulated that the retreat should not be further than the Moravian village, sixty-three miles distant from Sandwich on the Thames.

The Story of Tecumseh

CHAPTER XXIII.

THE RETREAT.

TECUMSEH had completely lost confidence in Procter. Immediately after the council he demanded a private audience with the General. During this interview, Tecumseh asked for a detailed statement of Procter's plan of campaign, pointing out that it was necessary that an advance force should set out at once for Moraviantown to make preparations for the reception of the main body and for the defence of the village. So evasive were Procter's replies that Tecumseh felt the British commander was deceiving him. He rose in a rage, and placing one hand upon the silver-mounted tomahawk in his belt, with the other struck the hilt of Procter's sword, exclaiming, " You are Procter, I am Tecumseh." Though Procter understood the challenge, he said nothing. Tecumseh stood for a moment gazing at the commander, and then, turning on his heel, stalked from the fort.

On the 20th of September, the wives of the officers with the women and children and the sick set out from Amherstburg for Chatham, Mrs. Procter and her daughter, who was ill, being in the company. They proceeded up the river in boats to Lake St. Clair and thence up the Thames to Chatham, where they were to await orders. Procter had apparently formed the opinion that Harrison would not follow him into the interior. He proceeded in the

OLD BARN, AS RENOVATED

Used as a field hospital at the Battle of Moraviantown

The Retreat

most leisurely manner to make preparations for the evacuation of Fort Amherstburg. Having sent away the women and children, his next thought was for the baggage. In direct breach of the regulations, he loaded a number of waggons with his own private property and that of his officers. It was not until the women and baggage had been despatched that he took thought for the transportation of the ammunition so vitally necessary to his army. These munitions of war were loaded on gunboats and bateaux, to be transported to the mouth of the Thames and up that river.

So dilatory was Procter that he was not ready to leave Amherstburg until the 24th of September. The torch was applied to the fort, the shipyard and all the public buildings. Leaving behind them this scene of cruel desolation, the army with Tecumseh and his Indians set out for Sandwich, the gunboats accompanying the retreat by way of the river. Harrison with almost five thousand men had arrived at Put-in Bay on the 22nd of September. He had ample means of transportation for this great army, having over one hundred craft of various descriptions, including a number of river gunboats. At Put-in Bay he was delayed by a severe storm on Lake Erie until the 27th of September, otherwise it is certain he would have reached Amherstburg before Procter had moved out. Procter lay at Sandwich until the 27th. Here he was joined by the garrison of Detroit. As the army moved out of Sandwich on its march to the Thames, they saw in the western sky the heavy pall of smoke which marked the destruction of Fort Detroit.

The Story of Tecumseh

On the same day Harrison's forces landed at Bar Point, three miles below Amherstburg, encamping for the night on a farm now owned by Edward Honor. With the caution which always characterized him, Harrison fortified his camp, throwing up temporary earthworks, the remains of which are visible to this day. On the next morning he marched into Amherstburg. As the Americans entered the town the fifes and drums struck up the tune of "Yankee Doodle." Smoking ruins alone remained to mark the site of the fort, the shipyard and the government buildings.

Harrison made no delay at Amherstburg, but pushed on to Sandwich. He found that the bridge over the Canard, the scene of the first engagement of the war, had been broken down by Procter's rear-guard. It was speedily repaired by the American engineers and the march continued, the entry into Sandwich taking place on the 29th. Colonel McArthur with seven hundred men was sent to occupy Detroit. Harrison, who was eager to pursue the retreating British, was forced to remain at Sandwich until the 2nd of October, awaiting the arrival of Colonel Johnson's regiment of twelve hundred mounted Kentuckians. Johnson had marched overland with the intention of joining Harrison at Amherstburg, but being delayed on the way, did not join Harrison until the latter had been some days at Sandwich. Having received these reinforcements, Harrison, with a force of over four thousand men, once more took up the pursuit in light marching order, all his baggage having been sent by water under the protection of three gunboats furnished by Commodore Perry, who accompanied the expedition.

The Retreat

Meanwhile, Procter proceeded on his leisurely retreat. In five days he had only covered fifty-four miles, reaching Dolsen's, or Dover, five miles west of Chatham, on the 1st of October. With an imbecility that passes comprehension he had not even taken the precaution to destroy the bridges behind him, and his rear was thus absolutely unprotected. Leaving Colonel Warburton in charge at Dolsen's, Procter with two hundred men, accompanied by Tecumseh and his Indians, rode to Chatham. Since leaving Sandwich the Indian force had dwindled down to one-half the original number.

Tecumseh strongly urged Procter to make a stand at Chatham, stating that he could not hold the Indians any longer. Procter agreed to examine the ground for the purpose of determining its suitability for defence. It was decided that a stand should be made at the point where McGregor's creek empties into the Thames, at the spot now known as Tecumseh Park, in the centre of the present city of Chatham. "Here," said Procter, "we will either defeat Harrison or leave our bones." As Tecumseh looked on the two streams which here commingled their waters, his thoughts flew backward to the home which he was destined never again to see. "This is a good place," said he. "It reminds me of my village at the junction of the Wabash and Tippecanoe."

The baggage and the boats containing the women and sick had already arrived at Chatham. The safety of these was as ever the first consideration with Procter. He therefore requested Tecumseh to remain at Chatham while he escorted the women and baggage to Moraviantown, promising to return before the enemy came up. When Procter reached Moraviantown he did not turn back. He sent the women and baggage forward accompanied by two hundred soldiers, instructing the officer in charge to continue his march until he reached Burlington. The sick, numbering one hundred officers and men, were placed in hospital at Moraviantown.

Tecumseh remained at Chatham awaiting Procter's return. Notwithstanding his utmost efforts, the numbers of the Indians steadily diminished. Roundhead, whose loyalty had never been above suspicion, now announced that he intended to return to Brownstown. Having waited one week without having heard from Procter, Tecumseh decided to consult Colonel Warburton, who was still at Dolsen's. Leaving his Indians in camp at Chatham, he arrived at Dolsen's on the 2nd of October, only to find that Warburton had received no message from Procter, and was in complete ignorance as to his whereabouts. The officers had lost all confidence in Procter, and urged Warburton to take over the command. Colonel Warburton learned for the first time from Tecumseh that Procter had promised to make a stand at Chatham. A council of war was immediately held, and it was decided to retreat to Chatham, there to await Procter's return. On the morning of the 3rd of October, a messenger galloped into Chatham with the news that Harrison's scouts had come in contact with the British rear-guard. Dispositions were at once made to resist an attack, and the allied forces lay all night under arms. Next morning raw meat was served to the troops, and as the hungry soldiers gathered round the

THE THAMES RIVER

Where the United States army crossed before the Battle of Moraviantown

The Retreat

fires, toasting the meat on long switches cut from the bushes, a second alarm was given, and the British again retreated six miles further to the eastward, where they halted for breakfast. Here they were joined by Procter. The retreat continued all day long. At Richardson's, six miles from Moraviantown, two companies were cut out as a rear-guard, and the main body proceeded to Sherman's, one mile further east, where they halted for the night. Tecumseh had refused to leave Chatham, and was much chagrined at Warburton for continuing the retreat.

Meanwhile, Harrison was approaching swiftly. By the end of the first day's march, October 2nd, he was twenty-five miles from Sandwich. Here he succeeded in capturing a small cavalry picket under Lieutenant Holmes. On the night of the 3rd he made camp at Drake's, four miles west of Dolsen's, and on the morning of the 4th advanced to Chatham. Tecumseh and his Indians had taken up a position near the bridge, and bravely contested Harrison's passage. So obstinate was the defence of the Indians that Harrison concluded that the whole British force must be in the vicinity. He accordingly halted until his guns could be brought into action. The artillery fire soon drove the Indians from their position, and Tecumseh reluctantly gave orders to retreat.

Reaching another bridge further up the river, Tecumseh, according to tradition, ordered his Indians to continue the march until they joined the British. He with two of his braves remained behind for the purpose of observing the enemy's movements. Tecumseh stood on the bridge with his right arm thrown over the neck of his white mustang, holding his rifle in his left hand, and thus awaited the Americans. Presently, around a bend in the road came Harrison's army. Tecumseh remained motionless, watching the advance of his foes. As they drew nearer, the Americans recognized the gallant figure which so audaciously barred their passage, and from a thousand throats arose a shout, "Tecumseh! Tecumseh!" A dozen horsemen rode out from the American lines and galloped towards the bridge. Tecumseh waited until the riders were almost upon him. Then, resting his rifle on his pony's back, he took deliberate aim and fired. The next moment he was clattering over the bridge, waving his arm towards his foes, who had now gained the approach. Riding at full speed down a cow-path, Tecumseh and his men soon distanced the pursuers. Emerging on the road, they made their way to the British camp at Sherman's. The Sherman farm, lot 15, concession B, township of Camden, lay along the bank of the river within the limits of the present village of Thamesville. The Longwoods road passed in front of the house, following the windings of the river to Moraviantown, four miles away. · It is a tradition in the Sherman family that young David Sherman, then a boy of fifteen, accompanied by a boy named Ward, were sent late in the afternoon of October 4th to bring in the cows from the bush. As they wandered through the woods they came upon an Indian seated upon a fallen tree. He wore a silk sash round about his head, in which was placed a large white ostrich plume. The Indian called the boys to him, asked their names and told them to get their cows and hurry home at once, for a

The Retreat

great many bad men would soon be coming down the road. When forty years later David Sherman laid out part of his farm in village lots, he named the village after that Indian—Tecumseh.

Harrison had continued his march, and notwithstanding the bad condition of the roads, for it had been a rainy season, made rapid progress. Shortly after he had crossed the bridge, one of Procter's gunboats, wreathed in flames, drifted by, and four miles further up the river, at Bowles's, two more gunboats, burning fiercely, lay against the bank. Attempts were made to extinguish the flames, but without success. Early in the morning of the 5th of October, Harrison had reached Arnold's Mills, where there was a ford. The river, swollen by the rains, filled its banks. The foot soldiers effected a crossing by clinging to the stirrups of the mounted men with one hand, while they held their muskets and powder-horns above the water with the other. Just above the mills two gunboats and several bateaux laden with ammunition were overtaken as they proceeded up this river under escort of one hundred and seventy-five officers and men of the 41st Regiment, the Newfoundland Regiment and the Royal Veterans.

The engagement that followed was of short duration, the boats were captured and the men taken prisoners, less than half a dozen making their escape. The captured boats contained all the ammunition and other supplies for the army. Through the inexcusable neglect of Procter, these boats with their invaluable contents had been permitted to fall behind in the retreat, while the commander directed all his energy to providing for the safety of his family and baggage. The fugitives bearing news of this disaster reached Procter's camp just as rations of raw beef, newly killed that morning, were being served out. Without allowing the troops to breakfast, Procter retreated eastward to a spot within two miles of Moraviantown and then made his stand. When Harrison arrived at Sherman's, the campfires were still burning. It was plain that the British were not far away. Harrison at once ordered Colonel Johnson's mounted regiment forward to locate the enemy. In a short time word was sent back that the British were formed across the line of march. The long pursuit was now drawing to a close.

Death of Tecumseh

CHAPTER XXIV.

DEATH OF TECUMSEH.

THE position of the Indian village of Moraviantown, situated on the north bank of the Thames, was one admirably adapted for defence. On the right a thick wood formed an ideal cover for the Indians; the left was protected by the river, while along the front extended a deep ravine filled with thick brush, so as to be almost impassable by cavalry, of which the enemy was known to possess a large number. A battery erected on the edge of the ravine could not be rushed, and from this commanding position would do great execution upon the enemy. For some reason, or lack of reason, Procter did not retreat to Moraviantown, but took up a position about one and a half miles west of the village, in a thick forest of beech, the ground at the point occupied by the troops being free from underbrush. Several changes of position were made without any apparent cause. The men, quick to note the indecision of their commander, complained that " they were ready and willing to fight for their knapsacks, and wished to meet the enemy, but did not like being knocked about in that manner, doing neither one thing nor the other." The same feeling pervaded the minds of the officers, but they checked their men.

It was now one o'clock, and the men had been without food all the morning. The only ammunition with which

The Story of Tecumseh

they were provided was what they carried in their pouches.
The wearied soldiers sat on logs and fallen trees beside
the Longwoods road. There were plenty of axes, but no
attempt was made to construct breastworks. Procter had
ceased to exercise the functions of a commanding officer,
and skulked behind the lines. His thoughts were with his
wife and sick daughter, riding through the woods towards
Burlington. He was, indeed, already a beaten man. The
little army, left without a general, resolved itself into
separate units under the command of the regimental officers. Under these circumstances there could be no con-
certed plan of battle.

Tecumseh, Shaubena and Calderwell were sitting
together on a log near the Indian camp, smoking their
pipes, when a messenger came to Tecumseh, asking him
to go to Procter at once. What transpired at that interview is unknown, but the chief soon returned, and, seating
himself beside his companions, silently filled his pipe.
After a long pause, Calderwell addressed Tecumseh:

"Father, what are we to do? Shall we fight the Americans?"

"Yes, my son," answered Tecumseh. "Before sunset
we will be in their smoke, as they are now almost upon us."
Unbuckling his sword, a gift from the British government,
Tecumseh handed it to Shaubena, saying, "If I should not
come out of this engagement, keep this sword, and when
my son is a great warrior, give it to him."

Presently the Indian scouts appeared running through
the woods. They brought news of the proximity of Harrison's army. On this alarm a portion of the 41st Regiment

Death of Tecumseh

under Colonel Warburton were ordered to form across the
road, their left resting on the road, which was here distant
about two hundred yards from the river, and their right
extending to a small swamp which ran parallel with the
river. The distance to be covered was so great that the
men were placed four or five feet apart. A second line
extended in the same manner at some distance in rear of
the first. Behind this second line General Procter took
his stand with his staff and a number of Provincial
Dragoons. On the road in front of this first line a
6-pounder had been placed, guarded by a score of Canadian light dragoons, but it was perfectly useless, as proper
ammunition had not been provided. Procter had placed
the other guns at a ford near Moraviantown, two miles distant from the battlefield. The ground between the small
swamp and another larger swamp was occupied by the
remainder of the 41st and a few men of the Newfoundland and Royal Veterans regiments. The Indians under
Tecumseh took up their position at the extreme right
within the border of the larger swamp. The total British
troops, including volunteers, numbered three hundred and
ninety-four. The Indians were reduced by desertion to
one thousand men, but they were all picked warriors
devoted to their chief. In this position the army remained
for two hours awaiting the enemy. Tecumseh, followed
by some of the lesser chiefs, passed down the lines to note
the disposition of the troops. He was dressed in his usual
costume of deerskin, the British medal hanging from his
neck. Round his forehead was bound a white silk hand-
kerchief, from which floated a white ostrich plume. He

The Story of Tecumseh

was in excellent spirits, shaking hands with the officers as he passed, and greeting his friends in the Shawanoe tongue. He then passed out of sight through the autumn woods to take his position at the head of the Indians in the great swamp. Passing along the front of the swamp on a final tour of inspection, he greeted the old warriors, telling them to " be brave, stand firm and shoot certain."

It was now nearly three o'clock. The moment for action had arrived. The bugle calls of the enemy already resounded through the woods. With clenched jaws and hands tightly clasping their muskets, the little army faced towards the foe, gazing down the vista of lofty tree trunks for a first glimpse of the enemy. Suddenly the woods before them were filled with horsemen. Colonel Johnson's cavalry, twelve hundred strong, swept down on the thin red line. On they came at full gallop, their cheers and shouts rising above the thunder of the pounding hoofs. Behind them the dank yellow autumn leaves were whirled in the air in the impetus of the charge. The riders, leaning forward in their saddles, were almost upon the British ranks when the order, " Fire!" rang sharp and clear down the line. A spurt of fire ran along the British front. Saddles were emptied and riderless horses dashed off into the wood. Here and there along the line of advance a horse went down, checking those who followed. Most of the horses, unaccustomed to firing, plunged and attempted to turn to one side. The confusion, however, was of short duration. Rallied by their officers, the American cavalry again formed and charged with irresistible force. The British front, not having had time to reload, fell back upon

Death of Tecumseh

the second line, which stood and fired an irregular volley. The next moment the enemy broke through the British ranks. The horsemen, wheeling and shooting to the right and left, beat down every show of opposition. The day, so far as the British were concerned, was lost. There was no alternative but to surrender. General Procter after the first volley sought safety in flight, accompanied by the dragoons. Though pursued by the enemy he managed to escape, arriving some days later at Burlington.

Harrison, beside four thousand white troops, had with him two hundred and fifty Indians. These he sent forward at the beginning of the engagement, directing them to steal through the woods between the river and the road to the rear of the British position, and then make an attack. This would lead the British to think that their own Indians had turned upon them.

While the British centre was being crushed, the Indians on the extreme right were giving a good account of themselves. Desha's Brigade attempted to dislodge them from the swamp. Concealed in the high marsh grass and behind clumps of wolf willow and fallen logs on the edge of the swamp, the Indians lay in wait until the Americans were almost upon them, and then a murderous fire was poured into the American ranks. The Longknives halted, fired a wavering volley and fell back upon Shelby's Brigade, which formed the centre of Harrison's line. The Indians, shouting their war-cry, emerged from the swamp intent on pursuing the retreating foe. Johnson's mounted regiment, having completely overthrown the British, were ordered to attack the Indians, and now appeared on the scene.

The Story of Tecumseh

Tecumseh at once retreated to the swamp, and sent word along the Indian front that they were not to fire until the cavalry were so near that the flints of their guns could be seen. Johnson came on in gallant style, expecting to ride through the Indians as easily as he had through the British. His horses were soon floundering in the bog. Tecumseh sprang up, shouting the Shawanoe war-cry. The painted warriors rose from their lair. Shrill and high rose the war-cries of a dozen nations in a wild discord which might well have appalled the bravest heart. A storm of lead swept the disorganized ranks of struggling horsemen. The front line was decimated. Wounded and dead lay on the trampled ground beneath the hoofs of the plunging horses. Colonel Johnson ordered his men to dismount and form on foot. Desha's Brigade moved up to the support of the Kentuckians. Together they advanced towards the swamp. The Indians maintained an irregular fire, discharging their muskets as fast as they could load. Though the Americans suffered severely from this galling fire, they would not be denied, but pressed on, determined to oust the Indians from their position. Tecumseh, for the purpose of encouraging his followers, exposed himself fearlessly. His mighty war-cry sounded high above the noise of battle. Suddenly he was seen to stagger and fall. Swiftly the words, "Tecumseh is dead!" passed down the line. Overwhelmed by this crowning calamity, the Indians turned and fled. The faithful bodyguard of the great chief carried the body of their dead leader deep into the recesses of the enshrouding woods. Down the dim forest aisles they bore him, and so he passes from the scene. The place of his

Death of Tecumseh

interment, kept a secret by his devoted followers, no man other than they has ever known. Like the shooting star for which he was named, he flamed across the sky and disappeared into the darkness. In the century which has elapsed since his death, his passing has become as legendary as that of King Arthur. The country for which he gave his life has raised no monument to his memory, but the great chief lives and will ever live in the hearts of men. Time has but added to his fame and made his immortality more secure. Wise in council, brave in war, humane in victory, and undaunted in defeat, the name of the great Shawanoe chief will go down to remotest history as that of the truest-hearted patriot, the ablest leader, and the most far-sighted statesman of his race.

> " Sleep well, Tecumseh, in thy unknown grave,
> Thou mighty savage, resolute and brave,
> Thou, Master and strong spirit of the woods,
> Unsheltered traveller in sad solitudes,
> Yearner o'er Wyandot and Cherokee,
> Could'st tell us now what hath been and shall be!"

SUPPLEMENT

So many versions of Tecumseh's death are given that it is practically impossible to determine which is correct. Major Richardson, who was present at Moraviantown, says: " Towards the close of the engagement he (Tecumseh) had been personally opposed to Colonel Johnson, commanding the American mounted horsemen, and wounded that officer with a ball from his rifle, and was in the act of springing upon him with his tomahawk, when his adversary drew a pistol from his belt and shot him dead on the spot. It has since been denied that the hero met his death from the hand of Colonel Johnson. Such was the statement on the day of action, nor was it ever contradicted at that period."

" The merit of having flayed the body of the fallen brave and made razor strops of his skin rests with his (Johnson's) immediate followers. This, too, has been denied, but denial is vain."

" Several of the officers of the 41st on being apprised of his (Tecumseh's) fall went, accompanied by some of General Harrison's staff, to visit the spot where Tecumseh lay, and there they identified (for they knew well) in the mangled corpse before them all that remained of the late powerful and intelligent chieftain."

" It has ever been a source of profound regret to me that I was not present at this inspection, for although the sight of the mutilated hero could not have failed to inflict on my heart pain of the most poignant kind, it would at least have been a consolation to have seen the last of his remains on earth, and this not more from the reverence and honour in which I had and have ever held the warrior than from the opportunity I should now possess of bearing attestation to the fact and manner of his fall from my own positive and personal observation."—*Richardson's " War of 1812"*

178

BLACK HAWK

The famous Sac Indian who joined the British forces in 1805

(From Nursey's "Legend of Pere Marquette")

Supplement

The story told by Shaubena, one of Tecumseh's bodyguard, corroborates Richardson.

It is rather extraordinary that Harrison in his despatches to the War Department at Washington announcing the victory at Moraviantown made no reference to the fall of Tecumseh.

One of Tecumseh's warriors was asked:
" What has become of Tecumseh?"
Raising the right hand to heaven, with an expression of sorrow,
" Gone."
" Did you see him on the day of battle?"
" Yes."
" When did you see him the last time?"
" Just as the Americans came in sight he, with his young braves, passed rapidly up and down the line, spoke to every old warrior, saw every one, said, ' Be brave, stand firm, shoot certain.' "
" Did you hear after the battle that he was killed or badly wounded?"
No answer.

—Hatch's " Chapter of the War."

" After withstanding almost the whole force of the Americans for some time, Tecumseh received a severe wound in the arm, but continued to fight with desperation until a blow in the head from an unknown hand laid him prostrate in the thickest of the fight. That the American soldiers should have dishonoured themselves after their victory by outraging all decency by acts of astonishing ferocity and barbarity upon the lifeless body of the fallen chief is grievous to mention, and cannot meet with too severe condemnation. Pieces of his skin were taken away by some of them as mementoes."—*Drake's " Indians of North America."*

As an example of the conflicting evidence regarding the circumstances of Tecumseh's death the same writer, Drake, in his biography of Tecumseh, contradicts his former statements, and states that Tecumseh was wounded in the hip and in the head. He denies the story that the body was mutilated by the Americans, but says that the body of a Pottawatomie chief was, by

179

Supplement

reason of his barbaric adornments, mistaken for that of Tecumseh. The Pottawatomie chief was scalped and the skin flayed from the body by the Kentuckians. Four Indians asserted that he was killed by the first fire, and four that he was slain by a horseman later on in the engagement. One Indian, Shaubena, stated that Tecumseh was shot in the neck, one that he was shot in the eye, two that he was shot in the hip, and two that he was shot in thirty different places.

"Colonel Richard M. Johnson with nineteen horsemen undertook to draw the Indian fire. Johnson had been wounded in four places but still kept the saddle, when a prominent chief fired his rifle at him, wounding him for the fifth time. His horse was also wounded so as to stumble, without, however, throwing its rider. Johnson had a pistol loaded with fine buckshot and a bullet. As the chief rushed at him with upraised tomahawk, Johnson fired. He must have reeled out of the saddle, for he remembered no more until hours afterward when he was told that he had killed Tecumseh. The friends of Richard Johnson positively asserted that he had slain Tecumseh, and the scene of the supposed exploit is graven on the monument to Johnson in the cemetery at Frankfort, Kentucky. Others, however, dispute the statement and maintain that it was another Indian whom Johnson shot and his Kentuckians mutilated."—*Coffin's* "*War of 1812.*"

"Two Indians were found on the field, and it was at first believed that one of them was Tecumseh, but later it was ascertained that his faithful braves had carried off their dead leader's body. The exasperated Kentuckians mutilated the supposed body of Tecumseh, and later Kentuckians have recorded by a sculpture in marble upon Colonel Johnson's monument in the cemetery at Frankfort their conviction that he killed Tecumseh."—*Lossing's* "*Cyclopædia of U. S. History.*"

"The Indian hero, Tecumseh, after being killed, was literally flayed in part by the Americans, and his skin carried off as a trophy."—*Bishop Strachan's letter to Jefferson.*

"A bitter and complicated discussion was long waged as to who killed Tecumseh. It is now quite impossible to decide the

Supplement

question; the conflicting testimony has hopelessly confused it. Many mistook the body of a gaily dressed and painted warrior for Tecumseh. It is a shameful fact that from this body much of the skin was stripped by some American frontiermen who had become as barbarous as the savages against whom they had waged a life-long warfare."—*Eggleston's " Tecumseh."*

The tradition handed down among the Indians is that Tecumseh was several times wounded, but fought on with blood flowing from his mouth over his deerskin jacket, until a chance bullet ended his life. When Tecumseh's voice was no longer heard the Indians lost heart and fled. They vehemently deny that the body was mutilated by the Americans, and affirm that he was carried into the woods and buried by his faithful followers, who took a solemn oath not to reveal the spot.

Lemuel Sherman, who lived on the Sherman farm, lot 15, concession B, township of Camden, in 1812, is supposed to have known where Tecumseh was buried, the spot having been pointed out to him by the Indians. The body, it is said, was carried by the followers of the chief a short distance east of the battlefield to the high ground at the back of the swamp. Here a large walnut tree had fallen and lay upon the ground. The trunk was separated in two branches. Between these branches the grave was made. Nearby stood a great beech. On this tree the Indians carved cabalistic signs, one of which was a Turtle totem. It is worthy of note that Tecumseh's mother belonged to the Turtle clan of the Shawanoes. In many of the Indian tribes it was customary for the children to take the totem of the mother instead of that of the father. Lemuel Sherman pointed out the tree to David Sherman, his son, the father of William Sherman, the present occupant of the farm.

One of Johnson's men, a Kentuckian named James Dunakey, remained with the Shermans until his death in 1857, and is buried in the Sherman cemetery. Dunakey stated that the Kentuckians, who were intoxicated at the time, had flayed Tecumseh's body. Dunakey fought under Wayne at the Fallen Timbers. During this campaign Wayne was closely pressed by the Indians, who declined to give battle, hoping to take the Americans by

181

Supplement

surprise. On one occasion, after having made camp for the night, Wayne ordered his men to cut logs about five or six feet in length. These logs were wrapped in blankets and disposed about the camp fires so as to resemble sleeping men. Wayne then withdrew his forces a little distance into the wood. The Indians were completely deceived by this ruse. Rushing into the camp they drove their tomahawks into the logs, whereupon Wayne from his ambush poured a deadly fire into their midst. On the night of his death the old Indian fighter, in delirium, re-lived his battles, rising in bed and shouting and pointing to his imaginary enemies.

The log house which stood on the Sherman farm in 1812 was located near the Longwoods road, about two hundred yards from the river, on the spot now occupied by the Sherman cemetery. Part of the framework was used in the construction of a granary. Near the house stood a frame barn which was afterwards moved to the back of the farm. This barn was used as a hospital after the battle. The beams still show initials carved by the soldiers. It has since been resheathed, but some of the original boards have been preserved. The Americans cut deep grooves in the boards so that they might tie their horses.

William Sherman has in his possession a military button found in the old orchard. The button is made of copper covered with silver plate and is the size of a twenty-five cent piece. The design is an eagle with spread wings bearing a scroll inscribed "e pluribus unum" in its mouth and grasping a fasces in its claws. On the upper part of the button are the words "United States Army," and below " ———Regiment," but the number of the regiment unfortunately cannot be discerned.

General Harrison on the morning after the battle ordered the settlers to assist in burying the dead. Lemuel Sherman assisted in digging a trench in which twelve bodies were placed. The slain were buried where they fell.

Carson Shaw, a descendant of Captain William Shaw, has in his possession a letter written from Dundas in November, 1813, by a man named Gowrie to Captain Shaw. Gowrie had been

BATTLEFIELD, MORAVIANTOWN

Looking north from Long Woods

Supplement

with Procter in the retreat from Amherstburg. He had left his
baggage at Fergusons, near Moraviantown, and wished to recover
it. He enumerates a large number of articles, silver knee buckles,
silver shoe buckles, a silver tea service, several suits of clothes,
etc. This throws some light on the charge made against Procter
at his court-martial after Moraviantown that his troops were
encumbered with a large amount of unnecessary and forbidden
private baggage.

The battlefield is about two miles from Sherman's, and is on
parts of lots 4, 5, 6 and 7 in the Gore of Zone, county of Kent.
More bullets and other relics have been found on lot 4 than on
the other lots. The Longwoods road runs along the front at a
distance of about one hundred and fifty feet from the River
Thames. At the east of the farm the river turns abruptly
towards the north, forming a bow, like the letter " U." A ridge
runs east and west across the farm parallel with and at a distance of about six hundred yards from the road. Along the foot
of this ridge the ground is low, being the site of the swamp
where Tecumseh and his Indians lay. When this swamp was
cleared the bones and skulls of a number of horses were found,
relics of Johnson's cavalry charge against the Indians.

There existed a tradition amongst the Indians on the Walpole
Island reservation that the body of Tecumseh was taken in 1864
from its original resting-place near the battlefield and re-interred
on St. Ann's Island, near Mitchell's Bay. It is stated that for
a number of years a British flag was kept floating above the
grave. A committee of Wallaceburg citizens determined to inves-
tigate the matter, and in May, 1910, went to St. Ann's Island.
With the assistance of the Indians the grave was located. Upon
excavations being made fragments of a box about three feet
square containing a skeleton in almost perfect condition were
discovered. A few of the smaller bones only were missing. The
size of the box and the position of the bones indicated that the
remains had been buried long after death. The Indians who were
present, after having withdrawn for consultation, permitted the
removal of the bones on the understanding that they were to
remain in the custody of Doctor Mitchell, a well-known physi-

Supplement

cian of Wallaceburg, in whom they had great confidence. A further condition exacted by the Indians was that the remains were to be delivered to them whenever demanded. Wrapped in the folds of the flag for which he gave his life Tecumseh's bones (if, indeed, these were the relics of the grat Shawanoe) were borne to Wallaceburg. Four days later the Indians obtained possession of the bones, and have since refused to disclose what has been done with them. Chief White has declared that they will return undisturbed to mother earth. Dr. Mitchell states that the skeleton was undoubtedly that of a male whose stature in life would correspond to that of Tecumseh, about five feet ten inches in height. Not being aware of the fact that Tecumseh, when a young man, had broken one of his legs, the Doctor made no special examination for indications of a fracture and did not notice any.

In a letter by Anthony Shane to Benjamin Drake (1821), Shane says "Tecumseh's son was called Pugeshashenwa, meaning ' cat in the act of seizing prey.' He was born in 1796. A grandson of Tecumseh was known as ' Big Jim.' He was chief of the Absentee Shawnees located in Oklahoma. He died in Mexico, August, 1901. A great grandson of Tecumseh, grandson of Pugeshashenwa (by a sister of Big Jim) was Thomas Washington, who was also an Absentee Shawnee chief. A few years ago some of the descendants of Tecumsapease (Tecumseh's sister) were still living in Missouri."—" Tecumseh," E. O. Randall, Ohio Archælogical and Historical Quarterly, October, 1906.

The Indians of Moraviantown belonged to the Delaware tribe and had lived on the Muskingum River, in Ohio, prior to moving to Canada. They had been converted to Christianity by the celebrated Moravian missionary, Count Zinzendorf, who had also preached to the Shawanoes. In 1781 and 1782 two separate raids had been made on the Moravian village on the Muskingum by bands of Kentuckians under Broadhead and Williamson. The Moravians were known as the "Praying Indians." They refused to take part in the border wars, and were a peaceable and inoffensive people. The "white savages" of Kentucky burned these villages and slaughtered the inhabitants—men, women and children. In one of these raids they surrounded the church in which

184

STONE TABLET

Marking the spot where Tecumseh fell at the
Battle of Moraviantown

Supplement

these Indians were praying and then set it on fire. Those who attempted to escape were either slain by the bayonets of the Americans or driven back into the flames. The remnant of the tribe sought refuge in Canada and established the village of Moraviantown, originally called Fairfield, on the north branch of the Thames. True to their religious belief, they took no part in the battle of Moraviantown. After the battle, when the Americans destroyed their village, the Indian women, it is said, threw their children into the Thames.

The site of the old village of Moraviantown is about one and a half miles from the battlefield. A few gnarled and twisted apple trees mark the spot. The ground has been dug up, probably by relic hunters. The present village is situated on the south side of the river. It is said that when the Great Western Railway was surveyed the Indians followed the engineers, watching the course of the road. It was thought that they were anxious to see that the remains of Tecumseh were not disturbed.

APPENDIX

No. 1.—FRONTISPIECE.

Tecumseh at the Battle of Moraviantown.

This is a portion of the painting reproduced in full on page 176, by Charles W. Jefferys, O.S.A.

No. 2.—FACING PAGE 11.

The Battle of Tippecanoe.

Reproduced from an illustration in a United States newspaper, from the original painting, by Chappel.

No. 3.—FACING PAGE 22.

Imaginary Portrait of Tecumseh.

By an unnamed artist. Reproduced from "Tecumseh, a Drama," by Charles Mair, the Canadian author.

No. 4.—FACING PAGE 35.

South Block House, Bois Blanc Island.

From a photograph, by F. Neal, of Sandwich.

No. 5.—FACING PAGE 45.

Attack on and Capture of the United States Flat Boats, on the Maumee River, Ohio, near Fort Meigs, in which Tecumseh as a Youth played a Conspicuous Part.

From the original oil painting in black and white, by Fergus Kyle.

186

GROUP OF WALLACEBURG RESIDENTS

At the opening of Tecumseh's alleged grave

Appendix

No. 6.—FACING PAGE 54.

Tecumseh Rescuing United States Soldiers from Indians.

From original water-color painting, by Charles W. Jefferys, O.S.A. This depicts Tecumseh's opportune arrival and rescue of the Kentucky, U. S., soldiers from the hands of the exasperated Indians at the fight near Fort Miami, where they had been taken prisoners.

No. 7.—FACING PAGE 67.

Shaubena, a Pottawatomie Brave, who fought under Tecumseh at Moraviantown.

Reproduction of the illustration in the "Legend of Père Marquette," by Walter R. Nursey. An antique bronze relief, by Edward Kemeys, the animal sculptor of "World's Fair" fame, in the rotunda of the Marquette building, Chicago.

No. 8.—FACING PAGE 76.

Plan of Harrison's Invasion of Canada, 1812.

From Casselman edition of Richardson's "War of 1812."

No. 9.—FACING PAGE 89.

Bust Statuette of Tecumseh.

From a photograph of the original bust, modelled in clay, by Hamilton MacCarthy, of Ottawa. This is, of course, imaginary. There is no authentic portrait of the Indian hero extant.

No. 10.—FACING PAGE 101.

Barracks at Fort Malden.

Now better known as Amherstburg, on the Detroit River, below Windsor, Ont. From a photograph.

Appendix

No. 11.—FACING PAGE 118.

Tecumseh and General Sir Isaac Brock Reconnoitring.

Opposite, across the river, stands Fort Detroit—formerly Fort Lernoult. To the right, on the Canadian side, is seen the tower of the fortification at Sandwich. This picture represents the Indian Chief and the British General on the river bank discussing the problem of the best crossing, which was made the day following, opposite Spring Wells. This illustration is from the original oil painting, by L. K. Smith.

No. 12.—FACING PAGE 123.

Plan of Detroit, 1812.

From Richardson's "War of 1812," by Casselman.

No. 13.—FACING PAGE 133.

Tecumseh and Brock at the Surrender of Detroit.

From the original water-color painting, by A. M. Wickson. This picture represents the two leading spirits of the drama when kept in suspense awaiting the return of Brock's special messengers, despatched to General Hull, with a demand for the surrender of Detroit. These messengers can be seen on the trail, conferring with Hull's despatch bearer, carrying a flag of truce. The incidents of the surrender of Hull and Detroit are also described in Chaps. XVIII. and XIX. of Nursey's "Story of Isaac Brock," the first volume of the Canadian Heroes Series, published by William Briggs, Toronto, of which the "Story of Tecumseh" is the companion publication.

No. 14.—FACING PAGE 139.

The Old Bâby Mansion (pronounced "Bawbee").

Was used as officers' headquarters at Sandwich during the campaign; the owner being a well-known merchant trader and loyalist. From a photograph of the renovated "mansion," by Neal.

Appendix

Appendix

relief, by Edward Kemeys, in the rotunda of the Marquette building, Chicago.

No. 22.—FACING PAGE 183.

The Battlefield of Moraviantown.

As it appears to-day, treeless, but cultivated, the old forest having long since vanished through fire, or by the aid of the settler's axe. Photograph by Neal.

No. 23.—FACING PAGE 185.

Tablet.

Marking the spot where Tecumseh is supposed to have fallen at Moraviantown.

No. 24.—FACING PAGE 186.

Group of Wallaceburg Residents.

Visiting the alleged place to which Tecumseh's remains are stated to have been taken after disinterment at Moraviantown. The bones unearthed at the spot on St. Anne's Island are positively claimed by the Indians to be those of the dead Chief. Though there is strong reason to believe this may have been the place of final sepulture, the story is shrouded in obscurity. There seems to be little likelihood of Tecumseh's last sepulchre ever being positively located.

Index

191

Index

Index

Index

Index

Index

CPSIA information can be obtained
at www.ICGtesting.com
Printed in the USA
LVOW13s2208190217
524769LV00004B/8/P